Margaret Reynolds has had a lengthy career in education and public policy working in Tasmania, London, Queensland and Canberra.

As a teacher she initially specialised in working with children with disabilities and expanded her professional interest to include cultural diversity, early intervention, Aboriginal education and teacher training.

Margaret was elected to the Townsville City Council in 1979 and the Australian Senate in 1983. She was a Minister in the Hawke Government 1987–1990 and was appointed the Australian Government's Representative on the Council for Aboriginal Reconciliation 1991–1996.

Margaret has represented Australia at a number of United Nations conferences and as Chair of the Commonwealth Human Rights Advisory Commission. Since leaving Parliament in 1999, she has taught Human Rights and International Politics at the University of Queensland and continued her human rights advocacy as National President of the United Nations Association of Australia.

She is currently State Manager of National Disability Services, Tasmania.

Living Politics

Margaret Reynolds

FOREWORD BY CARMEN LAWRENCE

UQP

First published 2007 by University of Queensland Press
PO Box 6042, St Lucia, Queensland 4067 Australia

www.uqp.uq.edu.au

Typeset in 12.5/16.5pt Bembo by Post Pre-press Group, Brisbane
Printed in Australia by McPherson's Printing Group

Cover painting: *Feminine strength: Portrait of Margaret Reynolds* (1990), by Glass, Bettina, 1930–. Acrylic on canvas, courtesy of the National Library of Australia.

Cataloguing in Publication Data
National Library of Australia

Reynolds, Margaret, 1941–
Living politics

1st ed.
ISBN 9780702234385.

1. Reynolds, Margaret, 1941–. 2. Australian Labor Party – Biography. 3. Women politicians – Australia – Biography. 4. Women teachers – Queensland – Biography. 5. Australia – Politics and government – 1965 –. I. Title.

324.29407092

FOREWORD

Dr Carmen Lawrence

The story of a trailblazer like Margaret Reynolds really needs no introduction or explanation; it speaks for itself. But, it is an honour to have the opportunity to comment on a political life of such substance. In some ways, the themes in Margaret's story are typical of those of many outstanding women of her generation: the broadening experience of education and the rejection of a dependent, second class status for women; a growing awareness of discrimination against our less fortunate compatriots; a painful realisation of the consequences of Indigenous dispossession and disadvantage; profound opposition to the militarism and violence embodied in the Vietnam war, a willingness to look beyond Australia's boundaries for inspiration and understanding and a fierce resistance to the unthinking embrace of the status quo.

What makes Margaret's story unique is that she managed all this in what many would regard as the least propitious environment for such a life – as a young mother in a remote, blokey town in northern Australia away from the comfortable supports of metropolitan life. Not only did she roll up her sleeves and take to the hustings with her kindred souls, but she did so knowing she was risking the criticism and ridicule which is so often directed at dissenters in small communities, and from which she knew there was no escape into the crowd. What is even more impressive is that Margaret came to have a genuine understanding and affection for the people of the north, even when she disagreed with them. And as a Queensland senator she was unstinting in pursuing their interests although, as she says, she felt she also had an obligation to sometimes reject and challenge community opinion and to act in accordance with her personal conviction.

Living Politics is the record of a feisty, resilient and independent woman with a love of life and a wry sense of the ridiculous. It was perhaps inevitable that such passionate and practical activism would ultimately lead to a successful and pioneering career in politics. Margaret Reynolds' sensitive antenna for injustice had its origins in her experience educating children with disabilities, a group for whom she remains a staunch advocate. 'I discovered', she says, that 'our society so often neglects its most vulnerable'. Her early campaign to 'normalise' the lives of disabled children and adolescents locked away in stifling institutions is the bedrock on which her ability to 'walk the fine line between independence and compliance' was based. She brought the same skill and her trademark enthusiasm to her later work in establishing early childhood programs for Indigenous children in Townsville and in campaigning to end the Vietnam War. As a young mother and teacher she became increasingly impatient with the patronising attitudes of those in authority and used this as a springboard to confront discrimination, refusing 'to meekly accept the word of men in power'. As an elected representative and Minister in the Hawke Government Margaret's direct and effective negotiating style broke down barriers of incomprehension and indifference.

Throughout her life in politics, Margaret revelled, as she put it, in 'trying to resolve the most intransigent problems' and although she came to understand the limits of political action, she has never stopped trying to make the world a better place.

Dedicated to all those people with whom I worked during my careers in education and politics – without you this story could not have been told nor would I have learned how politics affects so many aspects of our lives. And especially to my most supportive family who understand that the personal is political.

Contents

CHAPTER 1

Growing up in Tasmania 1941–1960

MY CHILDHOOD WAS profoundly affected by strong-minded women and by circumstances that taught me to be independent. I learned early that girls can do anything. My mother, Jess, established a self-reliant household where no task was considered beyond our combined capabilities. She used a hammer, paintbrush and axe with as much skill as she used a needle. Once, when visiting relatives, I unpacked a particular dress I disliked intensely and announced it was only for when I was chopping the wood! Of course I had never been allowed to use the axe, but I clearly imagined that one day this might be possible.

I was born in 1941 and grew up in the shadow of World War 2. I remember the celebrations in Hobart when peace was declared. I was in town with my mother and was amazed at the sight of all the people singing and dancing in the street, the car horns blaring and church bells ringing. I could not have understood what the celebrations were all about but the scene certainly made an impression. I did not really get to know my father, Rod Lyne, because he died soon after returning from service with the Australian Army in New Guinea. Jess and I then moved to Launceston where we lived just a few doors away from my maternal grandparents, Jessie and Robert Montgomery.

I remember my childhood with affection, though objectively my early life was disrupted by the impact of war. I knew my family situation was very different from others because I was an only child and grew up with a single, working mother. I cannot recall a time when my mother was not teaching. She returned to the work force when I was just three years old. During the war years when so many male teachers were on active duty the Tasmanian Education Department was desperate for teachers, so my mother was encouraged to take me to school with her. I started school at this early age, playing in the kindergarten and sleeping each afternoon while my mother taught the older children nearby.

I wanted a baby brother or sister and when I asked my mother she patiently explained the facts of life, but I reminded her that the Virgin Mary had managed without a husband. However, I grew up with friends, holidayed with cousins and came to accept my two-member family status. I seemed to have more freedom, special outings and holidays than most girls of my age. My family life was very casual because we did not need the rules required to manage larger families. I was surprised that my friends had to sit formally at a dinner table while my mother and I could eat by the fire or in the garden. An avid reader, I was even allowed to read during meals – a habit frowned on in most households.

Several of my friends had to look after younger siblings and were expected to do what seemed like an enormous amount of housework. I was expected to do my share of chores at home so I learned to use our shiny new vacuum cleaner and to cook simple meals on the gas stove. However, in my last year of primary school my mother employed a 'cleaning lady' and three nights a week we ate our evening meal at a nearby guesthouse. Such arrangements were unusual in a small Tasmanian town in the 1950s, but my mother was teaching and studying to upgrade her qualifications so this limited the time she had to spend on domestic routine.

Every afternoon after school was spent with my grandmother. I learned a great deal from her and I think she wanted me to have opportunities that had not been available to her. She encouraged me to think and talk about people and new ideas. I was very surprised when she suggested that in the future women may not marry because they would be working in their own careers. I was extremely doubtful about this because I was enthralled by the glamorous wedding pictures in women's magazines and thought no girl would forgo that one occasion to dress up like a princess. Jessie's own life experience had given her an unconventional view of women's roles in society and she challenged many of the traditional attitudes of the day. As a teenager my grandmother had developed blood poisoning and the country doctor advised her parents that she should have her leg amputated. Fortunately, my great-grandfather declared that no daughter of his would have such surgery, so instead she spent a lengthy period in hospital and recovered, but with a permanent limp. She became a junior teacher and for several years served her apprenticeship in country schools in northern Tasmania. A bicycle was specially adapted to suit her damaged leg, so she could cycle to work.

My grandmother kept me occupied after school with stories of her family life and I was especially fascinated by the story about my great-great-grandmother, Mary Bourhill, who had arrived in Tasmania with her father in 1854. The story was made more exciting because, at fourteen, Mary had run away to Gretna Green on the Scottish border to marry against the wishes of her father. When he returned from serving with the British Army in India, he apparently had forced his daughter to leave her new husband and sail to Australia with her parents to begin a new life in Tasmania. Mary's mother died en route and her dictatorial father also died soon after arriving in the colony. So Mary was alone in a strange country, no doubt grieving the loss of three close family members. She went into domestic service in a country house in New Norfolk and family legend has it that the son of the new settler tried to seduce Mary, so she left her job and set out at night on the long lonely walk to Hobart, more than 30 kilometres away. On the road she met a handsome young man, Charles Tomlin, and he gave her a ride in his buggy. They settled in Ellendale in the Derwent Valley and had fifteen children, the sixth being my great-grandmother, Martha, born in 1862.

My grandmother's story was incomplete; because when my mother later researched the family history she discovered our convict heritage. At sixteen years of age Charles Tomlin had been transported from England for stealing two watches. He met Mary when he had just received his ticket of leave to work as a free man in country Tasmania. My grandmother either did not know or did not talk about Charles's convict background. In the 1940s it was considered shameful to admit to a convict ancestor, but by the 1970s family history research had become a popular pastime for many people and my mother discovered several family secrets.

There is a fascinating sequel to my grandmother's story. When my great-grandmother, Martha Tomlin, had her first child (my grandmother) Jessie's birth is recorded with 'no father listed'. Like her mother Mary, young Martha had been in domestic service so she too may have experienced the attentions of her employer. We will never know if my grandmother knew the circumstances of her birth, but she certainly grew up wanting her daughters and granddaughters to have a great deal more control over their lives.

While I grew up to conform to the social climate of the 1950s,

I have no doubt that my attitudes were shaped by my mother and grandmother, who both encouraged me to have ambition and to be interested in the world beyond Launceston. I was a shy but quietly determined child who spent a lot of time in adult company. I had a vivid imagination and used to write adventure stories. I learned to play the piano and was often taken to concerts and the theatre to see local plays. I enjoyed considerable freedom to walk to the local primary school with my friends and we played in the bush, which led down the rocky slopes to the Cataract Gorge.

I attended the Trevallyn Primary School and spent Grades 5 and 6 in a composite class taught by the headmaster. Here I learned about the double standards applied to girls and boys. Most of the boys were frequently caned, yet the girls seemed to manage to escape the wrath of our teacher. Despite being a talkative child in class, I was often given extra privileges – I was allowed to read or draw with my friends outside in the garden or in the library. I could not have explained it then but in retrospect I know I also observed the way the headmaster favoured those of us who came from more privileged backgrounds. A number of my contemporaries were always being shamed as lazy and ignorant, yet it was actually their poverty which attracted this abuse.

I grew up listening to my mother and grandparents arguing about a man called Pig Iron Bob. My grandfather – a timber worker – talked about low wages, high prices and poor conditions for the workers. My mother seemed to agree with his assessment, yet my grandmother took the opposite view, respectfully praising a man called Mr Menzies! It was some time before I realised that they had been discussing the same person and that there was a clear division of political opinion in my family.

In 1952 all Tasmanian eleven year olds were required to sit an external exam known as the 'Ability Test'. It tested standards of literacy and numeracy as well as general knowledge, so I was lucky to have a schoolteacher mother who coached me to ensure I gained good results. Jess knew it was important I had the opportunity to go to the more academic high school rather than the alternative secondary modern school, where my options would have been more limited.

At Launceston High School I was taught by a number of delightfully eccentric women, most of whom were single career women. They provided me with the same kind of environment I experienced at home. Like my mother, they were professional women struggling for recognition in a male world. Yet they exuded a strength and confidence which was contagious. They taught in the humanities and their lessons often strayed into discussion of their personal experiences and travel, which particularly stimulated young women students. However, I did not enjoy the same level of confidence in maths and science classes, where male teachers so obviously doubted the capacities of girls and, like many girls of this period, I agreed with that assessment.

As I approached my mid-teens I became more strongly influenced by the standard expectations of my generation. I knew I would marry and have children, and hopefully my life would follow that fairytale portrayed by the Hollywood films of the day. Yet my own family's experience reminded me that some women might have to manage on their own, so it was important to be self-reliant. A number of my friends left school to stay at home and work locally, but my mother insisted that I should go away to university and it was inevitable that I would become a third-generation teacher.

I went to the University of Tasmania to complete a two-year teacher-training course. I was only sixteen and probably should have spent an extra year at school, but I had matriculated early and was keen to head off to Hobart with my contemporaries. I already had a university boyfriend, David. We had met when he came north on a sporting trip, so I was keen to develop this relationship. I was fascinated by David and his friends because they were so 'grown up' and talked earnestly about politics. I knew little of the detail but the debates seemed very impressive and I wanted to be part of this sophisticated world. Only several years later did I discover that the focus of their political discussions was the split in the Australian Labor Party (ALP) when the Catholic Church forced a breakaway group, which became the more conservative Democratic Labor Party (DLP). Little did I know at the time that a few years later I would join the ALP and be involved in some of the debates that resulted from the social conservatism of the DLP.

When I left home in 1958 I quickly discovered the excitement of life in the real world for young women of my generation. I neglected my studies to plunge headlong into a fascinating two years exploring my independence. I knew I should concentrate more on regularly attending lectures and completing assignments on time, but I was too busy enjoying myself. I joined the Old Nick Theatre Company to sing and dance my way through the University Revue production 'Fast 'n Lucifer'. I needed little persuasion to join the ranks of the lively campus scene. I drank underage but no one seemed to notice, and anyway I was determined to 'keep up' with my new friends.

When I started university I lived for six months in a young women's hostel 'Westella', but found the 10 pm curfew too restricting and launched myself into a series of moves to boarding houses and flats. I experienced my first harassment from a sleazy landlord when he came knocking on my door late at night demanding to come in for a drink. I was terrified because my room had French doors that opened on to a verandah, so I felt more vulnerable. After a few of these late-night calls I packed my bags, left one week's rent on the table and hurried away to join a girlfriend in a more secure flat in North Hobart.

Many of my contemporaries recall that these were the years when their political philosophies emerged, but I confess to having very limited development in this regard. I certainly advocated a form of equality in attempting to drink as much alcohol as my boyfriends, and I did resent the fact that only men had access to hotel bars. On one occasion I was part of a dare to 'chain' myself to a public bar to protest this discrimination, but sadly this action was much more social than political.

At the end of my first year at university I worked in the dining room of the Launceston Hotel, where I was initially interviewed about whether I could manage 'silver service'. I thought I knew all about this – after all, the cutlery was silver and I could set a table. Of course I was surprised to discover I was expected to serve vegetables to guests while manipulating fork and spoon in the one hand. Somehow I managed to bluff my way through the two months I worked there. On occasions I was asked to do 'breakfast trays', which involved delivery to the bedrooms. One morning I made my way up two flights of stairs with the heavy wooden tray, knocked at the door and waited. A male voice called out and I entered the darkened room but could see he was alone and was absolutely naked! He obviously enjoyed my discomfort because he urged me to bring the tray to the bedside table. I panicked, left the tray in the middle of the room and raced out the door. He even had the nerve to complain to my supervisor, who dismissed my version of events and said: 'Just remember the customer is always right'.

I first met Henry Reynolds at a university party in 1958. He was a rather loud, hard-drinking footballer with curly blond hair, kind eyes and a charming smile. He was friendly but rather superior because he knew I was fresh from school. Our paths crossed now and then, as it was a small campus. I was quite attracted to him but we were each in other relationships at the time so I didn't get to know him until about a year later. I had moved – again – to a small bed-sitter in West Hobart, unaware that Henry actually lived just around the corner at his family home in Knocklofty Terrace. One morning we met when we were both walking to the university. He was much more serious and quieter than I remembered him at parties. He even offered to carry my books! We started meeting this way on a regular basis and found we could talk easily about everything from local gossip to current affairs. One day he invited me home for Sunday night tea with his parents, Jack and Isabelle, and young sister, Judy, and I became a regular visitor. We became good friends, going to films and on long bush walks up Mt Wellington.

In 1960 I started my teaching career in a small Tasmanian farming community just out of Burnie on Tasmania's north-west coast. I was disgusted to be appointed to a school so far from my friends in Hobart. I even made an appointment to see the Director of Education to ask for an alternative placement, but he was obviously familiar with student teachers' pleas because he merely smiled and said he would review my eligibility in two years time. I was eighteen and convinced my social life had come to an end. I contemplated resigning and becoming a waitress in Hobart, but my mother reminded me I was a bonded student who would be obliged to repay the Education Department for my two-year teacher-training course.

So I reluctantly headed off to meet my commitments at the Natone Area School, where I was responsible for a large class of six year olds. I boarded with a senior teacher, Mrs Clarkson, her farmer husband and another young teacher. The small country cottage was very old, with few modern conveniences. I had to wash in cold water and was scared of the rats that occasionally strayed into my bedroom. However, I settled into the routine of spending five days in the country and travelling back to Hobart or Launceston most weekends.

From Monday to Friday we caught the school bus at 7.30 am and spent nearly an hour winding our way around the unsealed roads to collect children from all the farms in the Natone area. We repeated this journey each afternoon and spent many evenings preparing lessons for the next day. Once a week we played cards with my host family and their friends, when we stayed out late at sumptuous suppers and found it difficult to get moving the next morning.

I was always on the lookout for a ride to Hobart and sometimes I was lucky enough to find a colleague driving there. On other occasions I caught the bus or train, which had poor connecting services, so took much longer than by car. Despite the warnings I hitchhiked alone on several occasions and late one afternoon I found myself on a deserted road nervously waiting for a vehicle to come over the horizon. After nearly an hour walking in the dark a friendly middle-aged couple came to my rescue and I vowed to choose more reliable transport in the future.

I loved that first year teaching those young country children and tried to make my lessons interesting. I found the children to be at very different stages of development, a factor that had not been mentioned in my training. My headmaster, David Hunt, was a young progressive teacher who supported my efforts to introduce new ideas by purchasing educational toys, musical instruments and art supplies, none of which were standard issue at the time. Despite my job satisfaction, I still felt very isolated from my family and friends and I was determined to get a transfer back to Launceston or Hobart. My opportunity came when I read an advertisement seeking teachers to work in special education. David encouraged me to apply and within a few weeks

I was selected to do an in-service training course on teaching children with disabilities.

I was sent for a month to St Giles School for Crippled Children in Launceston, where I faced the harsh reality of my decision. I was shocked by the sight of so many children with such severe physical disabilities and doubted my ability to adapt to this environment. There was so much to learn about their individual conditions. I worried about my choice, which had been driven more by personal than professional priorities, and wondered how I would manage when sent to a school on my own. There were many demands on me in those few in-service training weeks so I was not given much time to indulge in self-doubt. I had made the choice to work with children with disabilities so I was just expected to get on with the job. In February 1961 I moved to Devonport, where I found private board with an elderly lady who lived within walking distance of my new school.

I was appointed teacher-in-charge at the special school in Devonport, where the Retarded Children's Welfare Association (RCWA) had established Devonfield – a combined school and hostel facility for children with intellectual disabilities. I was employed by the Tasmanian Education Department and its Special Education Unit in Hobart oversaw all aspects of my teaching and administration, but on a day-to-day basis I worked closely with the members of the RCWA and the house parents who were responsible for those children who lived on the premises.

By this time Henry Reynolds had been transferred to the region to teach at the high school in Burnie, which was just a half-hour bus ride from Devonport. We began meeting at weekends to re-create our student lifestyle in country Tasmania. We smoked and drank to excess and I stayed overnight in Henry's flat. We were old friends learning to become lovers and ultimately this would lead to a lifetime partnership.

CHAPTER 2

Discovering politics 1961–1963

DEVONFIELD WAS LOCATED on a slight hill in Middle Road, Devonport, and was surrounded by bush. It was a low-set L-shaped building with a small residential wing and a school area that included a large classroom, office and toilets. The hostel accommodated six intellectually disabled country children and an additional twelve youngsters from the Devonport region attended school as day students. I had one assistant – a magnificent older woman, Judy Poltock, whose school-age daughter had suffered serious brain injury as a result of being born without medical support during a London air raid. Judy was a genial, practical individual who had learned from personal experience how to relate to intellectually disabled children. It was her good humour and spirit of optimism that helped me launch into my new job.

My role involved expanding the enrolment at the school and promoting the still-new educational idea that children with intellectual and physical disabilities *should* go to school. I was the only 'trained' teacher at Devonfield so I was expected to take a leadership role by setting priorities, planning the educational program and promoting the school throughout the community. In between times I was also responsible for teaching a group of children who had many complex educational needs. The Retarded Children's Welfare Association wanted me to be an advocate and publicist for them, because fundraising was essential to further develop Devonfield and to finance a new separate school building. After school and in the evenings I worked with the local committee and attended meetings of other community organisations to promote understanding of my work with intellectually disabled children. I became a regular guest speaker at service clubs and soon realised that personalising the stories of the children created increased awareness of this new field of special education. I told stories about the seven year old taught his first words by older disabled children and the four year old encouraged by her friends to use her walking frame.

In the early 1960s it was unusual for a young woman to be invited to address men-only service clubs, but many groups wanted to find out more about fundraising for Devonfield. On one occasion I fronted the local Lions Club and tried to respond appropriately to the sight and sound of a room full of middle aged men 'roaring' – a custom which was part of this organisation's regular dinner routine.

I loved the independence of my new role, unencumbered by the specific demands of the classroom within the regular school system. I thrived on the challenge of trialling new ideas and methods of engaging my students. In the 1960s children with disabilities were still hidden from the world by parents ashamed and fearful of their children's differences. Many children were misdiagnosed and could have been integrated into the general classroom, but at this time it was official policy for children considered handicapped to be isolated in special schools. But only a few special schools had been established in Tasmania so it was not unusual for children with intellectual disabilities to be denied access to any form of schooling, particularly in country areas.

So many people thought these children were poor victims unable to help themselves, let alone each other. At this time handicapped children were viewed with sympathy, but many were not expected to live very long so the general attitude was one of either avoidance or pity. But I only knew a lively group of kids who had the capacity to be happy, sad or mischievous. They liked to play and sing and avoid schoolwork just the same as other children. I enjoyed presenting this fresh impression and found it easy to talk about my work, explaining the reason for the developments in special education. I remembered my initial response to the physically handicapped children at St Giles and used my new-found confidence to encourage people to better understand disabled children and how important it was for them to have access to education.

Enrolment increased during my first year so the Education Department gave approval for me to appoint a junior assistant. I also organised a team of volunteers to come to the school to supervise cooking, craft and woodwork. The new school building was completed and we were able to move to the new site in 1962.

My work highlighted the need to normalise the lives of 'special' children and I began organising visits out into their community. Initially this new idea was met with considerable opposition from some of the parents who feared the children would be ridiculed or harmed by the experience. The Education Department was convinced it would be too great a risk to enable children to go beyond the grounds of their protected environment. Just a few parents were very supportive and helped me organise after-school outings. I began by taking a small group to visit the fire station and this successful outing led to other excursions into town and to the beach. So I was slowly able to encourage permission from all parents. This gradual process of 'normalisation' was of considerable benefit to the youngsters and started to break down barriers within the community.

In 1962, my second year at Devonfield, I organised a five-day holiday camp at the National Fitness Council camp at Port Sorell. For most children it was their first time away from home, and for their families it was a unique opportunity to allow their children to enjoy a new-found independence. I wanted to involve other children from the nearby primary school so that intellectually disabled children could participate in a more integrated environment. I approached the school's headmaster and asked if this might be possible. He obtained permission from a number of families and several eleven year olds joined us for the week's camp.

The camp was run by a National Fitness Council officer, Tony Andrikonis – an easygoing young man who successfully involved all children in a range of games, walks and campfire singsongs as well as camp chores like peeling vegetables, sweeping and washing up. The camp was the first of its kind in Tasmania, so created considerable media interest. We posed for photographs and I did interviews with journalists who interrogated me about taking children away from the 'safety' of Devonfield. The Tasmanian Film Corporation sent a film crew to make a short documentary of the initiative and it was subsequently used in educational training. I was very pleased that the camp attracted this kind of attention because it validated my efforts to change attitudes towards children with disabilities.

My work at Devonfield was beginning to focus my attention on human rights and public policy. I started to recognise the discrimination that families of children with disabilities faced. Many doctors in the 1960s were ill-equipped to diagnose and effectively advise on how to manage the lives of children with specific disabilities or developmental delays. Children with major conditions like cerebral palsy, Down syndrome, brain injury, autism or hearing and sight loss were not expected to lead normal lives. Members of the medical profession tended to concentrate on the parents, preparing them for a lifetime of full-time caring. A number of health professionals were quick to recommend institutionalisation 'for the sake of the rest of the family'.

Parents welcomed the new facility for their children at Devonfield Special School because it gave them some respite for a few hours a day, but they were still angry with a health and education system which had been slow to provide schooling for their children. There was considerable frustration about their experience of insensitive bureaucracy. Not surprisingly, when parents found that their child was to be placed in the care of a mere twenty year old with no experience of child-rearing, they were anxious and suspicious about my ability to cope with the demands of the job.

However, gradually those parents who had thought me irresponsible for suggesting their children could engage in normal activities like visits to the local library began to see their children as individuals, responding to new challenges. In the social environment of the early 1960s parents were not encouraged to have any expectation that disabled children were entitled to the same opportunities as other children. There was no official recognition of discrimination and the human rights discourse was very distant from my life as a country schoolteacher. Yet it was this training ground that made me aware that the inability to understand difference can lead to some people's life chances being considerably reduced.

My two years at Devonfield introduced me to the reality of working with government. I had yet to acquire an understanding of the politics of decision making, but my initial experience of bureaucracy was quite bewildering. No one in the Tasmanian Education Department ever explained how to work within an administrative hierarchy. There were the written rules, which were complex, but the unwritten rules were incomprehensible. It was not easy to innovate, yet working with intellectually and physically disabled children in the 1960s required teachers to be proactive and inventive in providing educational opportunity. I was often frustrated by departmental guidelines which did not recognise the day-to-day challenges I faced working with limited resources, so on several occasions I decided to ignore the regulations and just focus on the children. I soon discovered decisions could be made by advising my superiors after the event! This could have been disastrous for my career but fortunately I managed to walk that fine line between independence and compliance, a lesson that has served me well over many years. I began to understand how to work for change in a society that routinely discriminated against some of its most vulnerable members.

In 1963, after two years at Devonfield, I was transferred to a very different environment within Tasmania's major mental health institution, Lachlan Park – a collection of red brick and sandstone buildings set in parkland and located in the Derwent Valley at New Norfolk, about thirty-five kilometres from Hobart. While Devonfield was an open facility – a modern building complete with garden and playground – Lachlan Park was a secure mental asylum surrounded by a high wall, its main entrance dominated by forbidding iron gates and a gatehouse with security guards to ensure that only the authorised entered or departed. At Devonfield many children enjoyed family life, whereas Lachlan Park was considered to be 'the dumping ground' for children whose families had despaired – giving up their children to institutional care because they received no advice or support about caring at home.

Lachlan Park catered for all types of patients – young and old – many of whom spent their lifetimes locked away from the world. Some suffered from mental illness, while others were incarcerated as medically 'insane'. They were the abandoned victims of a society that could not accommodate their difference. Eccentric or disruptive behaviour led to their certification under the Mental Health Act. These people had no rights as citizens or even as human beings.

I approached my new job at the Lachlan Park Special School with some trepidation. I discovered that the school itself was fully enclosed within the grounds of that notorious nineteenth-century institution, commonly known in the local community as 'that mad house'. As the new teacher-in-charge I was issued with a large master key which opened the security gates throughout the institutional complex. I was instructed to wear it constantly on a chain – like a gaoler. Apparently it was essential to protect this key as it was supposed to be impossible to move around between buildings without opening locked doors and gates. However, an enterprising young pupil, Tom, soon became my personal gate monitor, unlocking the formidable gates with a 'key' he had made from a wire coathanger. He was very proud of his ability to help me, so I could not dampen his enthusiasm. Like so many institutionalised children he craved recognition and his 'key' was his way of demonstrating how he had adjusted to his closed environment.

The school itself was a former hospital ward – cold and dark. The furniture was basic and the equipment minimal. My assistants had attempted to brighten their surroundings with pictures and children's paintings, yet on my first visit to the school I could see only a drab room with limited natural light. The playground was empty and had high steel bars separating it from the exercise yards of male alcoholic patients on one side and young offenders on the other. In that cold and dank schoolroom, which smelt of hospital disinfectant and stale boiled cabbage, I seriously doubted my ability to create a learning environment.

I was again employed by the Education Department and had two assistants to work with the sixteen children who were formally enrolled. The hospital also assigned two women patients to work in the school's kitchen and to clean our schoolroom. One was a severe woman very critical of the children and, I suspect, of the new teacher. She was a refugee from Central Europe, her World War 2 experience having shattered her psychological wellbeing. On several occasions her delusions overwhelmed her brusque manner and I would find her cowering in the toilet re-experiencing the horrors of aerial bombing. Her co-worker was a nervous, smiling woman who loved the children and cried for her two daughters who had been removed from her care when she was hospitalised during a nervous breakdown. Both women should have been released back into the community, but neither had family prepared to accept them and there were no other options at that time.

I had no background in understanding mental patients and I suppose I could have found it difficult to adjust to working alongside older women who had experienced such trauma in their lives. However, both women knew their routines and I was grateful to have their assistance so they came to accept the newcomer and I adjusted to some of their unpredictable ways. So many women patients in Lachlan Park in the 1960s shared their backgrounds. They were women traumatised by war and relocation, where cultural difference led to misunderstanding and neglect. I also knew some young women patients diagnosed as having a 'mental illness' purely because their families did not understand their behaviour and so had them certified unnecessarily to 'protect them from themselves'.

If I found the location of the school depressing, then my first visit to the large Children's Ward would reinforce my shock at the conditions in which so many handicapped children were living. It was a separate building close to the entrance of the institution. In the Children's Ward nursing staff did their best to care for up to forty girls and boys from birth to ten years of age, but they were inadequately trained to cater for the physical, mental and emotional needs of young children. Some children were reluctantly institutionalised and their parents visited and took them for outings. However, many families were encouraged to leave their children in the care of the state and to forget about them.

I discovered that there were a number of factors affecting whether or not children could attend school. Firstly, it was left up to the nursing staff to decide if youngsters were 'bright enough to learn anything'. As so many children had spent years without any stimulation it seemed to me scarcely surprising that they appeared to lack ability. However, at this time it was still believed to be a waste of time and money trying to 'educate' retarded children. Secondly, many children were physically disabled and some were incontinent, so it was assumed that their specialised needs could not be met in a school environment. Thirdly, the Education Department was actually intent on relegating its responsibility to the Health Department. A small school unit within a major health facility was seen as highly inefficient so it was *not* the Education Department's goal to increase enrolment. Finally, most doctors within the institution had labelled the children of Lachlan Park 'ineducable'. Some of the files I read dismissed individuals by simply labelling children with one word – 'imbecile'. Nursing staff corroborated this by describing the children's behaviour as either 'withdrawn' or 'hyperactive'.

The Children's Ward was a very dispiriting place. It contained rows of cots and narrow iron beds, but there was no colour or life in the room. The floors were regularly mopped with standard hospital-issue disinfectant so the air was thick with an overpowering smell. Several young children suffering varying degrees of paralysis or mental retardation were confined to their beds. I was appalled to discover that many of them were actually tied down with bandages, their bodies lifeless and their expressions vacant. Nurses were initially hostile about my presence, viewing me as an interfering outsider. They obviously resented my quizzing them about children whose conditions they knew to be 'hopeless'. It seemed very few people bothered to ask about these children because no one expected their condition to change.

I could not accept that these children should be left in bed day after day with no stimulation or experience outside the Children's Ward. I wondered about other children and teenagers in this large institution and began to visit other wards where older children lived. Most girls over ten were in adult wards in a more modern section of the hospital. However, many of the boys over ten lived in a separate secure ward in the care of male nurses. Some staff members were genuinely fond of 'their boys', but the sound of beatings was not uncommon. The school was located adjacent to the Boys' Ward, so too often I heard boys crying out as a result of violent punishment. Many of the young males within the Boys' Ward were juvenile offenders, detained with disabled youngsters because Lachlan Park was then Tasmania's only secure location apart from Risdon Prison. Forty boys of all abilities and ages lived together in an environment with few opportunities to be involved in any meaningful activity. I got to know many of them as they wandered aimlessly in their enclosed yard, peering forlornly through the bars and asking when they could come to school.

The atmosphere of the Children's and Boys' Wards was disturbing, but nothing could have prepared me for J Ward – a maximum security ward for some of the most disabled adult female patients. J Ward was located in the oldest section of the hospital. It was built by convict labour and reflected all the worst features of nineteenth-century institutional design. I may never have been allowed into this high-security area but one of our pupils, a thirteen-year-old girl, had been transferred there from the Children's Ward. Jenny was a disturbed child but not lacking in intelligence. She had fits of violent anger – often directed at younger children – and 'wandered' from less secure wards, so had been placed in this stark environment where the exceptional and volatile behaviour of older patients put her at considerable risk. At school Jenny's behaviour could be managed, as she enjoyed reading and writing. She complained bitterly about her transfer to J Ward, commenting with insight well beyond her years: 'I don't like being there locked up with all those old mad women. I'm not mad like them, I'm just slow and nobody wants me.'

It was obvious why Jenny punished younger children, as she herself had been rejected by parents unable to manage her behaviour within a large family. She associated her treatment with the apparent preference of her parents for her younger siblings, so she hit out at any young child. Despite many efforts to highlight Jenny's inappropriate placement in J Ward, she remained there for several months living with the mentally ill and the medically insane. She witnessed the extremes of behaviour and observed the routine treatment of the era, regularly reporting to me in graphic detail the effect of electric shock treatment on some patients: 'I heard her screaming "no – no more" but they took her into that cruel place with the wires and I couldn't hear her anymore.'

I used to visit Jenny after school because she needed extra support and some respite from the quite manic environment. Whenever I went into J Ward, I was approached immediately by women of all ages screaming, sobbing or laughing hysterically as they gesticulated in my direction. They craved human attention and affection, so it was impossible to bypass individuals without being hugged and kissed. Yet the physical condition of many women was quite offensive as some were incontinent and others regularly tore at their clothes and rejected efforts to maintain basic cleanliness. The ward smelt of urine and faeces, so it was difficult to breathe normally in the putrid atmosphere. Some women lived in a world of their own, sitting on the cold stone floor in foetal position, rocking backwards and forwards as they hummed a long-forgotten tune. Others ran at the wall, banging their heads in an alarming manner, while others wandered waving their hands distractedly towards the light from outside. These were the discarded women of Lachlan Park, hidden by a system that could do no more than feed, clothe and house them. Only a few were discharged from J Ward, but many remained drugged and disinfected until the day they died.

Some days Jenny was not allowed to come to school because nursing staff used this as a punishment. On occasions her violent temper led to conflict with older patients, but it was her placement in this totally inappropriate setting that created most of the problems. When Jenny was kept in the ward I would take her schoolwork to try to provide some activity for her during the day. Whenever I visited she was always pleased to see me, but I was even more relieved to see her so we could retreat from the main ward to a small, enclosed veranda where some attempt had been made to isolate this child from other patients in the day room. I worked hard to have her transferred from J Ward to a more suitable environment but she had a bad reputation, having attacked several nurses in her fear and frustration. Senior nursing staff could not believe that Jenny was a well-behaved child when she was allowed to come to school. She had her own routine and responsibilities, successfully completing a range of school and craft work. Finally, after weeks of conflict culminating in Jenny being beaten up by other patients, I took her case to the Medical Superintendent, Dr John Weatherly. He was equally disturbed by the precedent of allowing this young girl to live in such an extreme environment and directed that she be immediately transferred to a more open ward, where she blossomed in her new, relaxed environment. I was amazed that the resident medical superintendent had been unaware of Jenny's plight and for the first time realised how remote senior authorities can be from the reality of life for people in their care. The institution was like a small village, with up to 1000 patients, so Dr Weatherly did not always know of the disturbing practices within the hospital. However, he was very determined to change the culture of Lachlan Park, so I could actually challenge the system and receive a positive response.

In those early months at Lachlan Park, I saw the worst features of institutionalisation, but also learned to work in the positive atmosphere of a community trying to change. There were many kind and committed staff working long hours in nightmarish conditions. Some 'adopted' particular patients and offered daily affection and humour to cheer up the grim reality of institutional life. But the culture of despair pervaded the entire hospital. It was not a place for children to live and develop their potential. Nevertheless, while recognising that the school could only alleviate some of this isolation, I knew our efforts were important in attempting to bring some normality into the lives of these children.

I again approached John Weatherly, who was attempting to open up Lachlan Park to new ideas and practices, and asked his permission for up to sixty additional children to start attending school. He was delighted because he wanted to see the Education Department accepting greater responsibility for schooling within his institution. The existing staffing and allocated space were inadequate for such a dramatic increase in enrolment but I was confident of finding a way to manage these limitations. I suggested to him that the school could provide sessional classes so that children attended school for at least one hour a day. Dr Weatherly gave approval for nurses to bring children to and from the school at intervals during the day. He instructed hospital carpenters to make some building modifications so they converted a school storeroom into a playroom for three and four year olds. The local branch of the Retarded Children's Welfare Association supported the Lachlan Park Special School, so we launched a community appeal that resulted in the donation of an array of colourful soft toys for younger children. Nurses brought children to school in wheelchairs and on mobile beds. I began to experiment with music and massage therapy without really understanding these methods. There was little information and no equipment available for me at the time, so my teaching assistants and I learned to be inventive in trying anything to gain some response from small children who had become accustomed to lying or sitting patiently awaiting the next meal or toilet routine. We sang and danced and turned ourselves into clowns to encourage that first glimmer of understanding. I asked nursing staff to try some of our ideas and we sent pictures and toys back to the Children's Ward to provide a little more interesting environment. Some older nurses were sceptical about all this fuss over children going to school but others were keen to work with us. I was invited to give some lectures to nursing staff because Dr Weatherly wanted to see more activities initiated within hospital wards. Gradually we were able to show that all children could learn something, given time and encouragement. No one was more excited by this than the children themselves, who started smiling and attempting language. Nurses and medical staff reviewed their earlier diagnoses – we had convinced them there was no such word as 'ineducable'.

The school was offered the use of an old wooden hall not far from the main schoolrooms, so it became a base for my class of teenage boys. We acquired tables and chairs from the hospital store and had woodwork benches installed by the local committee. The boys' chronological ages ranged from eleven to twenty-one, but their mental functioning age was considerably lower. Many had never learned to read and my initial effort with conventional curriculum materials was largely unsuccessful. However when one boy, Geoff, brought a copy of the Melbourne *Truth* to school there was suddenly a greatly increased interest in reading. Newspapers were supposed to be banned from Boys' Ward, but Geoff had managed to get a copy from one of the other wards. He wanted me to read an article about his uncle, who had been gaoled for car theft, and after I had read the detail he carefully copied the words to make up his own story, which he read back to me.

Each morning I bought copies of newspapers and they became much-valued teaching aids for these young men who wanted to know what was going on 'outside'. It was surprising just how quickly they learned to read from the sporting pages and court reports. Each day individuals worked on their selected news story and these 'illiterate' youngsters began reading and writing about events that interested them. The boys responded well to a range of new opportunities and freedoms provided at school. They learned to cook and take on responsibility for working with younger children. We introduced woodwork, art and sport, each supervised by male patients from the alcoholic rehabilitation ward adjacent to the school. I did not face any problem behaviours because the boys regarded school as such a welcome escape. Of course they were noisy and high-spirited but they saw that I was responsible for giving them an opportunity to get away from the boredom of ward life. I was only a few years older than several, so I think they regarded me less as an authority figure and more as a big sister. They also knew the ultimate punishment might be exclusion from school, but I never needed to implement such a threat.

The school became a focus of attention within the institution as both staff and some patients began to change their attitudes and help the children to enjoy school life. Despite having many of the negative features of a 1960s' mental hospital, Lachlan Park was also a community of people who wanted to see improvements in the lives of their patients. They could see the way even the most disabled youngster was benefiting from the experience of educational activities. The behaviour of many older boys originally denied access to school had radically improved so even some of the male nurses who had been responsible for violent punishment were generous in their praise. It was a rewarding time to be part of such a supportive community.

However, there was still little awareness or understanding of these changes within the Education Department. I may have had allies at Lachlan Park, but my employer was still treating the school as an inconsequential unit of sixteen children. Enrolment had more than trebled, but still there was no response to my repeated requests for additional staff and equipment.

One evening I conveyed my frustration to friends Rosalind Wesley and her husband Harry Holgate who, as an astute political journalist with the *Examiner* newspaper, immediately recognised a good story. I agreed to his visit to the school, believing that any publicity would benefit the school's fundraising efforts. However, I was unprepared for the response to his article, complete with photos, in a double-page feature headlined 'New Hope for the Forgotten Children of Lachlan Park'. I should have realised that it was unacceptable for an obscure young schoolteacher to organise such a fanfare of publicity, especially as it implied criticism of the Education Department. While I had been relatively circumspect in my comments, Harry recognised the reality of government neglect. Suddenly there was a buzz of enquiry from the head office in Hobart.

Everyone wanted to know what was happening at the Lachlan Park Special School. I received dozens of requests for information and visitors from government departments started to appear unannounced. Questions were asked and forms had to be completed in triplicate. A new teacher was appointed and equipment started arriving by the truckload. With the attention came increased scrutiny of some of my more unorthodox methods. It was difficult to explain to a school inspector that it was perfectly safe for me to be in the same room as a dozen young men and their carpentry teacher. My volunteers from the Alcoholic Treatment Ward had no formal qualifications as instructors, so it seemed all departmental guidelines had been breached. Yet the school was functioning very well and so many children's lives had been transformed.

Fortunately, both the Head of Special Education, Paul Morrow, and Dr Weatherly fully supported my unconventional efforts so I was protected from some of the more zealous enquiries. Meanwhile, Health and Education Department officials were still arguing about areas of responsibility and which budget would cover the new demands created by increased enrolment at the school. One day Paul phoned to tell me that 'even the Minister had asked for a briefing'. At the time I was so politically naïve that I assumed this query must have come from one of the many ministers of religion who visited Lachlan Park! I did not follow the processes of government decision making and initially could not understand why the Minister for Education would be asking about our school. I had stumbled into a political debate I didn't fully comprehend, but by chance had waged a campaign which opened up new approaches to teaching within this institutional environment.

I finished teaching at Lachlan Park in December 1963 to marry and travel overseas. My three years experience of working at Devonfield and Lachlan Park was personally formative in ways well beyond my teaching career. It was in those years I learned a great deal about people and the choices they are able to make. I discovered our society so often neglects its most vulnerable citizens and I learned how public policy develops. I didn't realise it at the time, but I had embarked on a course of trying to change the way we respond to those who are different. The language and practice of human rights and politics would catch up with me several years later. But I believe it was the children of Devonfield and Lachlan Park who opened my eyes to discrimination and injustice.

CHAPTER 3

Marriage and a new world 1963–1965

Henry and I married on 20 December 1963. We had been engaged for twelve months, but kept up appearances by living separately. We had spent several holidays together, booking into hotels as a married couple – the status then expected of couples sharing a double bed. However, we scandalised the local postmistress at Eaglehawk Neck on Tasman's Peninsula, where we had rented a cottage for a summer holiday. My mother wrote to me care of the Post Office and addressed the envelope 'Miss Margaret Lyne'. My single status had been revealed, and whenever we went to the adjacent shop we were received with such obvious disapproval that we believed everyone in the small community had been told of our transgression.

Most of our contemporaries expected to marry and settle down a few years after establishing themselves in the work force. We wanted to travel overseas together and, even though we regarded ourselves as progressive in our attitudes, it would have been unthinkable that we leave our families to 'live in sin' – that censorious description given to cohabiting unmarried couples.

Despite my grandmother's pronouncement that in future some

women may choose not to marry, I wanted to be a bride and have the service in a lovely old church with family in attendance. So we chose St Mary's Anglican Church, built in 1861. It is the final resting place of Sir Richard Dry, the first premier of Tasmania, who was a vocal opponent of convict transportation. Ours was a small family wedding followed by a reception at Fitzpatrick's Inn in Westbury, about 30 kilometres from Launceston.

As neither of us drove in those days we left our reception on the regular evening service of the Green Coach Line bus. As we boarded the bus our relatives threw confetti, much to the amusement of other passengers. We spent two days on the north-west coast and flew to Melbourne to embark on our overseas adventure aboard the Italian liner *Castel Felice*. We had each been to the mainland before so were familiar with both Melbourne and Sydney, but the real excitement was in boarding the big white ship and joining hundreds of passengers for an Italian smorgasbord on our first night at sea. The array of beautifully prepared food was almost as appealing as our introduction to Asti Spumante, an Italian sparkling wine we could buy very cheaply.

Our first port of call was Sydney on Christmas Day, when mainly quiet English migrants left the ship for a new life down under. They were replaced by more vocal young Australians heading off on their overseas working holidays. We took the ferry to Manly, where we found very few shops open but finally bought takeaway chicken for lunch. On return to the ship we were treated to a gala Christmas dinner, more Asti Spumante and late night dancing at the nightly cabaret. A day later we stopped in Brisbane, where we found it to be overwhelmingly hot and I tried to cool down by paddling in the King George Square ornamental pool. However, a stern Queensland policeman reprimanded me and ordered me to replace my sandals. As we travelled north we saw the lights of Townsville, completely unaware that we would return there to live for more than thirty years.

For five weeks we lived in a tiny cramped inside cabin with only artificial light and too much luggage because I had insisted on bringing not only three suitcases, but a beach bag complete with umbrella, a tartan rug, a picnic set and a hat box. I am not sure why I took such an assortment of items for two years travel overseas. The cases had to be stored so we could actually get in and out of our cabin.

Our long-term plan was to teach in London and we had already sent details of our qualifications to the Inner London Education Authority. However, we also had vague ideas about working in Italy so planned to leave the ship in Naples, laden down with all my worldly possessions.

In the 1960s it was not an option to travel by plane, as it was far too expensive. Young Australians like us travelled by boat, taking weeks to cruise to the northern hemisphere enjoying lazy days by the pool and partying at night. But the most exciting part of the long journey was arriving in 'foreign' ports. The first stopover in Singapore was our introduction to another world. The *Castel Felice* anchored offshore and dozens of Singaporeans came alongside in their tiny boats to show us what they had for sale. Before the ship was ready for passengers to disembark they clambered aboard, bringing an array of craft goods and mechanical toys as they wandered along the decks. We bargained through gestures and their halting English and bought trinkets we would never have dreamt of buying except in such exotic circumstances. We were then allowed to go ashore in larger boats, which ferried us from our floating home to the wharf, and then we were able to explore for the day. It was such a teeming, bustling environment unlike anything we had experienced. It was also our first introduction to this kind of poverty so when a couple of street urchins approached us we were eager to offer our Australian coins, which meant that quite a crowd of kids followed us around the narrow streets.

We lunched at Raffles in colonial splendour, fascinated not only by the elegant surroundings but also by the fact that we had four waiters to attend to our every need. We smoked between courses and found we only had to fumble for our cigarettes to have a waiter with lighter immediately at our service. Later in the day we rode in a rickshaw; two sturdy westerners pulled along by a slight young man who ran along crowded streets to show us the sights. At one point we found ourselves in a non-tourist area surrounded by suspicious locals as we tried to view an open-air Chinese opera. They stared and pointed at us and our guide was eager to return us to the security of an area closer to the centre of the city.

While five weeks at sea enjoying an excellent range of Italian food and wine in a holiday atmosphere was very attractive for a time, we did get bored with the long sea voyage. We really looked forward to the break in routine when the ship docked for refuelling and supplies, so we could spend a day exploring another new environment. It was an era when travel gave immediate access to other cultures without the distraction of Coca-Cola or McDonald's. When we left the ship we were immediately immersed in totally different worlds in which every image, sound and smell was so unfamiliar. We wandered the crowded, dusty streets of Singapore, Colombo, Aden, Port Said and Cairo where much of the life of the city was conducted outdoors. One of the special interests of our days in port was exploring the markets and spending too much on a variety of items we added to our excess luggage. In Colombo Henry bought me a beautiful white embossed sari and a 'sapphire' bracelet we thought was a great bargain until we discovered years later it was just cut glass. In

Aden I was shocked after queuing at the toilet to discover it was an open space with several women of various ages squatting over holes in the ground.

We left the ship in Port Said for the day and then went by bus through the desert landscape to reach Cairo. It was here I first saw soldiers patrolling the streets armed with submachine guns and, although the city held the same fascination as others we had explored, I had a sense of insecurity about this country where there were ongoing tensions over British access to the Suez Canal and there seemed a heightened atmosphere of distrust. Our buses were held up for over an hour while passengers were scrutinised and passports rechecked. It may have been nothing more than inefficiency in managing large numbers of tourists, but I was certainly glad to return to the familiarity of the ship.

When we arrived finally in Naples we realised that our dream of wandering freely to perhaps tread grapes somewhere in an Italian vineyard was quite impractical, because we had arrived in the middle of winter. However, we checked into a charming *pensione* with a balcony overlooking the city and began to plan our travel in Italy. We walked the back streets of Naples and went by boat to the Isle of Capri but soon appreciated we had to think seriously about how we would continue to fund this lifestyle. We thought we might earn some money teaching English so decided to travel to Rome, where we made an appointment to be interviewed at the Berlitz School of English Language. However, our self-confidence was considerably eroded when we were asked how many languages we spoke and had to confess to just high-school standard French and German. We were told in no uncertain terms that Berlitz only employed multilingual teachers.

We spent a week in Rome and then decided to store our luggage at the central railway station so we could travel with just overnight bags to Florence and Venice. We had membership of the Youth Hostels Association and knew it would be cheaper to stay in hostels. In Florence we checked in to separate dormitories at a youth hostel in a castle just out of the city, but Henry spent a sleepless night with noisy American backpackers boasting as they showed off their handguns. After his somewhat traumatic experience we abandoned this way of saving money and moved to a delightful hillside hotel in Fiesole. It was surrounded by cypress trees and our room looked down on the rooftops of Florence. We fell in love with both Florence and Venice, spending our days admiring the art and architecture and our evenings eating pasta and drinking the local wine in small cafés. After a couple of weeks we knew we simply had to get to London because we had almost exhausted our savings and had to face the reality of finding permanent accommodation and employment. We returned to Rome, collected our stored luggage on a trolley and caught a train across Europe. The further north we went the more the landscape was shrouded in mist as we left behind the bright blue skies of Italy.

We arrived in London on a cold, damp evening in February 1964 and stayed overnight in a grubby, rundown hotel near Victoria Station. The next morning we scanned the newspapers for accommodation and were able to find a one-room bed-sit in a pleasant house in Willesden Green, about twenty minutes ride on the Underground train from central London. The room was too small for us but we were promised two rooms within a few weeks when another tenant moved. Our first London home had a small bedroom and a living room/kitchen overlooking a large garden and it became our base for that first six months in England.

We were unable to start teaching until after the Easter school holidays, so we started looking at all the suburban notice boards and newspapers for casual work to replenish our finances. I applied for several advertised jobs in hotels and theatres and was offered a job as an usherette in a West End cinema, the Astoria, on the corner of Oxford Street and Tottenham Court Road. I wore a drab brown uniform with gold braid trim and sat through endless screenings of *The Cardinal*, a religious film made more memorable by being set in Rome. Soon after I started I heard that our theatre was to host the Royal Premiere of *The Fall of the Roman Empire*, with the Duke of Edinburgh in attendance. My colleagues were eager to find out who would be chosen to show this special guest to his seat. When the young Australian was given the job there was considerable hostility towards me. My workmates had much more experience, so were naturally resentful. I was given a new, more attractive cream uniform which actually fitted, and was promoted to working in the dress circle.

On the big night I arrived early to find the theatre already surrounded by crowds of people anxious to get a glimpse of Prince Philip. I hurried in through a side door, changed and was sent upstairs to wait for the official party. When the royal entourage of about six people arrived I had to walk ahead and stand at the end of the front row until the prince and his guests were seated. While I was being given instructions for this important duty there had been some debate about whether or not I should curtsy. I had no intention of embarrassing myself by conforming to this strange ritual but fortunately it seemed this was only expected if the Queen herself had been in attendance. Having successfully steered British royalty in the right direction, I was then free to stand and watch the glamorous audience arrive in their furs and diamonds. I was agog at the sight of so many elegant people, the women dressed in fabulous satin evening gowns and the men in dinner suits. More than twenty years later Henry and I met Queen Elizabeth and Prince Philip at the opening of the new Parliament House in Canberra, so I had the opportunity to remind the prince of our earlier 'meeting'.

While working at the theatre I earned just £7 a week, which barely covered meagre provisions and my transport to and from central London. Henry could not get work as potential employers assumed he would go teaching within a few months, so he gave up trying and was confined to our suburban bed-sitter because my wage did not provide any extra money for him to travel into the city. He spent nearly two months in the Willesden Green Library reading every art book in their collection. Our kindly Indian landlord trusted us to repay some back rent when we became well-paid schoolteachers and we adapted to life without cigarettes, alcohol and fresh food. We discovered baked beans and tinned fish and became accustomed to life on a limited income, which was quite a contrast to our easy-going days in Tasmania.

After the Easter school holidays we both got jobs teaching in the East End and started to earn enough money to get out and enjoy the city. We negotiated the London Underground to find our way around and visited all the major tourist attractions, from the Tower of London to Westminster Abbey. One day we went to Hampstead Heath where we stopped for afternoon tea at Kenwood House, a gracious nineteenth-century National Trust house. We could have had our tea in the café, but I insisted we join the well-dressed English ladies in the elegant drawing room overlooking the park. The rather snooty waitress seated us in a distant corner, presumably because our casual clothes did not meet the standard of this establishment. She was slow to serve us and by the time our tea and scones finally arrived I was very annoyed by her attitude. I attempted to pour the tea from the attractive china teapot and discovered there was something blocking the flow. I lifted the lid and saw to my horror a small, dark brown object caught in the spout. 'It's a dead mouse' I complained to Henry and with a grand gesture I called the waitress to report this alarming discovery. She came to our table and I announced what I had found. She lifted the teapot lid and said with absolute disdain: 'Madam, that is a tea bag'. We hurriedly finished and left, with me grumbling that for the cost of this special treat I had a right to expect real tea!

Within a month of settling in London, I discovered I was pregnant and was shocked because I believed totally in the reliability of the contraceptive pill. I had been one of the first young women in Hobart to be given the revolutionary new contraceptive by a doctor who had written out the prescription several months before we married, earnestly telling me I should start taking the pill before my wedding 'so my system could adjust to married life'. I was not sure what he meant, but was informed enough to welcome this new form of contraception. In London several months later I remembered that during our travels in Italy I had neglected to take the pill for a short time because I had left my next month's supply stored in the Rome railway station. When calculating dates we decided our firstborn would have the distinction of knowing he was conceived in a small hotel on the Grand Canal within the sound of the bells of St Marco.

This pregnancy was not part of our grand plan and I had qualms about admitting to Henry that 'my' carelessness may have disrupted our working holiday. In the 1960s only young women were responsible for contraception. We were conditioned to expect men to resent having their freedom curtailed by unexpected pregnancy and I accepted that assumption. It was the era of 'shotgun' marriages when couples felt obliged to make their relationship legal, but the prevailing attitude of the day 'blamed' women for failed contraception. I announced my condition to Henry the night the doctor had confirmed my suspicions. He was excited by my news but thought I may want to go home to Tasmania for the birth. However, having been assured that Henry was quite accepting of our new circumstances I couldn't see that there were any problems with having a baby in London.

The free British national health system had already set in train all necessary support services. After just one visit to the doctor I had a bed booked at the North London Kingsbury Maternity Hospital for my delivery date in November and was also enrolled for antenatal classes there. I was given all relevant forms to complete, including one which resulted in two cash grants to help purchase new baby requirements. My doctor sent me home with coupons that entitled me to free milk and orange juice for the duration of my pregnancy. We were most impressed with this introduction to British health care.

I had a smooth pregnancy and continued to enjoy the cultural life of London. We discovered Covent Garden, queued for cheap tickets in the amphitheatre, and went to opera and ballet up until just days before John's birth. We saw the magnificent Zefferelli productions of the operas *Rigoletto* and *Tosca* and were treated to renowned singers like Tito Gobbi and Joan Sutherland. We watched the magical performance of Margot Fonteyn dancing with Rudolph Nureyev just after he had defected from the Soviet Union. In this period we were able to be in the Royal Albert Hall when the veteran conductor Otto Klemperer gave one of his last concerts. We also saw the young cellist, Jacqueline Du Pre, together with Daniel Barenboim at Festival Hall, and Richard Burton at the National Theatre. We visited galleries, museums and the grand country houses of the British aristocracy. It was a wonderful opportunity to be able to access so much theatre and be inspired by the cultural life of a world city.

In the July summer holidays we travelled by English Channel ferry to the Netherlands and in Amsterdam stayed with a Dutch family offering bed and breakfast to tourists so they could engage in conversational English. We took a cruise down the Rhine, stopping at Koblenz and then went by train up the Moselle Valley to the small town of Cochem, where we had great difficulty finding accommodation until a kindly couple took pity on my obvious pregnancy and offered us a small attic room in their home. We explored the vineyards though unfortunately only Henry could indulge in the wine tasting.

When we returned to London we moved to a small Georgian terrace house owned by a journalist, Bertha Gaster, who was on assignment for six months in Hungary. She had advertised in the weekly journal *New Society* for booklovers to care for her extensive library. The two-storey cottage overlooked the Grand Union Canal in Islington and was surrounded by postwar high-rise apartments. Each day we travelled by train and bus across North London to our schools in Hackney and Dalton.

Henry taught at a tough East End secondary school – in his first few weeks, two boys fighting with broken bottles confronted him. But the Cockney youngsters related well to young Australians who did not have the airs and graces of middle-class English teachers. My school was known as the Stormont House School for Delicate Children, a halfway house for children leaving hospital or referred to the school because they had specific medical conditions. The school's focus was a healthy diet and we seemed to spend half the day in the well-appointed dining room where breakfast, lunch and high tea were major occasions to be supervised by teaching staff. The school had its own cook and school nurse, who together planned well-balanced meals unknown to many Cockney families in the 1960s. It was in this environment that I was introduced to spotted dick, toad in the hole, brains and tripe – all chosen for their nutritional value. This enhanced diet, which we teachers were expected to enjoy, obviously contributed to the very healthy son I produced later in the year.

The school may have been identified with 'delicate' children but I found their language and general demeanour quite the opposite. Many of the older girls and boys were sexually active and openly gossiped about their experiences. A number of girls had helped deliver younger siblings in home births so they gave me graphic descriptions of what to expect in labour. While I enjoyed teaching the predominantly Cockney and West Indian children, there was little challenge in the work and on occasions I felt guilty about being little more than an overpaid babysitter. I continued teaching until October 1964, when I left teaching to prepare for our baby's arrival.

John was a healthy, nine and a half pound baby but, because he was born in the winter following the big freeze of 1963 when many babies and elderly people died, we were required to stay in hospital for ten days. I was in a large public ward and, while there was certain regimentation about baby care, the hospital seemed to be well managed and staffed. Breastfeeding was not encouraged and within a few hours of John's birth I was handed a swaddled baby and a bottle of infant formula, one of up to a dozen or so being distributed. When I whispered to my neighbour about my preference for breastfeeding she was quite dismissive of the idea, but when her five children visited her I better understood her attitude. I conveyed my concern to a helpful young nurse who confided in me that she had fed both her children, but the hospital was provided with formula and staff found it easier to discourage 'old fashioned' breastfeeding which required individual support. Fortunately I managed, with her assistance, to be one of only a few women in the ward to rely on natural feeding.

Returning home with our precious bundle was quite traumatic after all the horror stories about the risks to winter babies. While our small house was warm enough I was quite paranoid at first about venturing outside. I had borrowed a large old pram – the kind wheeled by nannies in Kensington Gardens – and would stop every few minutes to check that the sleeping child was still breathing. Gradually I became more relaxed about the awesome responsibility of caring for this small infant. Henry seemed to have more background knowledge about babies, having grown up with a younger sister and niece, so his advice and assistance were greatly appreciated.

One late winter's afternoon I had just settled John in his cot upstairs when there was a knock at the front door. There had been several gangland murders around the Kings Cross area near us so I was rather reluctant to open the door, but told myself Henry had probably forgotten his key. There on my doorstep was the darkest stranger I had ever seen at such close quarters. I was extremely nervous about his unannounced presence but also concerned that my reaction was more extreme because of his colour. I was ashamed of my irrational response to his dark skin so, to cover my embarrassment, I promptly invited him in and offered him a cup of tea. He was a West Indian student waiting for our neighbour who tutored him in English and by the time Henry arrived home we were chatting like old friends. It was an experience I have often described in later years when encouraging people to talk about prejudice.

In the early months of 1965 I was preoccupied with caring for John. I enjoyed long walks to different parts of London, exploring areas of the city still devastated by World War 2 bombing and watching new building developments around St Paul's Cathedral. I shopped in the lively Chapel St market and went out every morning to sit with other mothers at the local launderette. I felt really at home with my domestic routine in London. At weekends Henry and I used public transport to take John out into the country, swinging the carrycot between us as we walked. We made friends with an Australian couple, Pat and Rob Inglis, who were well established in London with their two children. They encouraged us to leave John with them so we could continue to go out to the theatre at night. John adapted well to various new environments so this experience taught us that having a baby did not necessarily confine us to home.

When John was four months old I was asked to return to my old teaching job at Stormont House and it seemed the obvious thing to do. We were living on just one wage and really needed the extra income if we were to continue to travel and enjoy life in London. Unlike many of my friends back in Australia I didn't have any feelings of guilt because I had grown up with a working mother and it seemed only natural that I would return to teaching. My only concern was finding good child care, so we chose a Cockney neighbour, Mrs Rogers, who also cared for two other small children at home. John was introduced to 'family day care' and Henry and I embarked on a lifestyle that ultimately would lead us to juggle three children, two careers and a great deal of community activism.

Joint parenting was an unknown concept at the time and had we produced our firstborn in Tasmania the pattern of our child rearing may have been very different. Our generation assumed that child care, especially of very young children, was the sole responsibility of mothers and female relatives. It was common practice for the women of the extended family to converge on the new mother, offering support and advice. In these circumstances fathers were effectively 'locked out' just at the very time when they were needed to provide practical fathering – changing nappies, bathing, settling a crying baby – as well as providing reassurance and emotional support. In London, away from family and with mainly carefree Australian singles in our circle of friends, I relied totally on Henry as the other parent and together we shared child care from the outset. This was a significant factor in our being able to continue developing an equal partnership in our marriage almost a decade before many Australian women questioned their partner's responsibilities in child rearing. Long before I had heard the feminist debate about sex-role stereotyping or read about Swedish analysis of the changing roles of men and women, the circumstances of two young innocents abroad in London initiated a way of life that became central to our marriage and family life.

In August 1965 Henry was offered an academic position at the Townsville campus of the University of Queensland, starting as soon as possible. It was an important opportunity for his career and, although we were very happy living in London, we had only a few months remaining on our working visas so knew we had to soon leave the United Kingdom. We were also very eager to introduce John to our families and friends back in Tasmania.

Henry's university contract included our first-class travel aboard the *Galileo*, another Italian ship that sailed from Genoa, so we took the opportunity to return to Italy for a final week's travel. We flew to Rome and went by train again to Florence, this time travelling with a pram and juggling the demands of a baby. Italy is ideal for travelling with small children; and everywhere we went people wanted to nurse or play with John. We almost lost him in a Rome department store when shop assistants took him from counter to counter to be admired as an unusually blond infant for that region.

Our cabin on the return journey was much grander than the one we had on the *Castel Felice* and had a view of the deck and endless ocean. We called very briefly at Naples, Messina and Djibouti but John and I did not disembark because there was limited time in each port. Our days were spent reading, swimming and amusing John, who was also able to spend a few hours a day in the ship's crèche. As first-class passengers all our extras were billed at the end of the voyage, so by the time we reached Fremantle we were becoming very nervous about our cash flow.

It was strange spending a day in Fremantle after nearly two

years away and the first thing we noticed was the Australian accents, which sounded so broad and unfamiliar. Fremantle itself seemed extraordinarily quiet and almost deserted because we had become accustomed to crowded overseas cities. We finally disembarked in Melbourne and flew home to Tasmania, where we spent a few weeks with family in Launceston and Hobart. Old friends greeted us as if we had never left but we found our time overseas had changed us. We no longer related to the local scene and the small town atmosphere actually seemed quite restrictive. When we unpacked we discovered that a collection of art postcards Henry had bought at various galleries and museums in our travels was missing. Apparently over-zealous customs officers had taken offence at several nude images including Michelangelo's *David* and the entire collection had been seized. We had arrived home just in time for the censorship debate about what adult Australians could view and read!

Henry headed north to Townsville alone to find accommodation and settle into his new job. He wrote me several letters over the three-week period and his initial response to the northern city was rather negative. The overwhelming heat and a plague of cockroaches featured prominently. He warned me to get used to the idea of living in a small, isolated provincial city with few public facilities. I remember him calling from a phone box opposite the Cootharinga Home for Crippled Children. He said I might get a job there because 'you will have to get involved in something or you will go mad up here!' A few days later I spent an entire day bundling baby and luggage on to several flights as we made the long flight up the Australian coast from Tasmania to reach the North Queensland tropical city that would shape my life for the next three decades.

CHAPTER 4

Life on the Queensland frontier 1965–1969

My first memory of Townsville was of waking early to sunshine streaming in the window and hearing a strange tropical birdcall. At 6 am it was bright and hot under the mosquito net, which was such a contrast to the chill of English winter. The scene from the window of our North Ward flat was quite remote from any in my experience – the pink granite of Castle Hill caught the early morning sun, casting a rosy glow on the rock face. The surrounding suburb was dry and flat, with weatherboard houses perched high above the ground on stilts. It was quiet and deserted – a very different environment from either the familiar comfort of Tasmania or the recent excitement of London.

That day Henry and I walked along the Strand beachfront, amazed to see such a vast expanse of empty sand and sparkling water. But my calm and scenic introduction to Townsville was shattered as we turned the corner into Flinders Street in the city centre. Women and children scurried past the numerous hotels where men congregated, and the swinging doors worked overtime as drinkers swaggered in and out of the crowded bars.

We had never encountered such a public display of masculine bravado. The main street was reminiscent of a set for a western movie. Shopping in this frontier town constantly reminded us of our isolation as we discovered that fresh fruit and vegetables were scarce and the choice limited. In setting up our new home we found that many basic household items had to be ordered from Brisbane and we waited for weeks for them to be freighted up the Bruce Highway.

The city centre itself was very busy and crowded with people and we immediately noticed the cultural diversity of North Queensland. In 1965 the town's Aborigines and Torres Strait Islanders made up close to 10 per cent of the population, with many families living in the city centre and nearby suburbs of South Townsville, Railway Estate and West End. Their presence impressed us, as newcomers, but it soon became clear that they were ignored or shunned by most locals. In the 1960s numbers of Aborigines had moved to the coast from western cattle stations to get work on the railways and the council road gangs, or at the meatworks. Many station owners had refused to accept the outcome of the Equal Wage Case of 1965 – that the same wages had to be paid to both black and white stockmen – so they no longer employed Aborigines in large numbers. At the same time Torres Strait Islanders left the islands to work in the urban centres of Cairns, Townsville and Mackay to provide better opportunities for their families. There was also considerable movement between Palm Island, the largest Aboriginal reserve in Australia, and Townsville with people travelling regularly by boat to the city.

When we made the decision to leave London to come to North Queensland, we had imagined Townsville as a lush tropical city similar in size and facilities to my hometown of Launceston, but with the very appealing bonus of perpetual summer. We were unfamiliar with the geographic reality of Townsville's location in a 'rain shadow', or with a tropical climate that divided the year into just wet and dry seasons. Our first impressions were disappointing as we focused on the parched landscape and discovered it would not rain for another four months. At that time Townsville's infrastructure suffered from neglect because of its isolation. It was a poorly serviced city of unsealed roads, no footpaths and only basic services. The airport, even though it was a major defence base, had only a tin shed as its main public terminal.

The heat and dust seemed to affect every aspect of our lives in those first few months. A plague of bush flies covered the net of John's pram whenever I walked to town. We wondered if we had made the right decision, but youthful enthusiasm carried us forward as we began to explore our totally new environment.

Townsville was a working-class town but had an elite of professionals who had campaigned to get a university campus in North Queensland. As newcomers to the university community we found it was assumed that the almost all-male staff and their wives would create their own social circle. Within weeks of our arrival I was asked to join the 'Staff and Distaff Wives Club', so named to make a clear distinction between academic and administrative staff. I was welcomed to this group at a morning tea held in Townsville's Queens Gardens. On my arrival I was astonished to find that most other women were dressed in formal linen frocks, their outfits complete with stockings and hats better suited to a wedding or garden party. I was very casually dressed in sundress and sandals and baby John looked positively neglected beside the other beautifully dressed children. I had not thought that such a morning tea would be an occasion to dress so formally but in conversation I learned that, although we were living in the tropics, it was important to 'keep up appearances'. I thought this strange as the climate was far too hot for me and the mere thought of stockings had me sweating more profusely.

Everyone was very friendly and solicitous about how I was settling in yet the lively chatter was a world away from my interests and experience of living in London. It seemed several women were unhappy about being so far away from their extended families, but felt it was their duty to support the careers of their husbands by living in this remote part of Australia. I was already thinking about returning to work at least part time, but it was clear that my new acquaintances were full-time wives and mothers. It seemed from some of their comments that, as the wife of an aspiring academic, I was destined to just support Henry's new career and manage an efficient household.

I was quite happy with my status as a young wife and mother but felt there had to be new opportunities for me personally. Most Australian women in this era were expected to concentrate on their family responsibilities and not become distracted by their own ambitions. Having grown up with a working mother this was not my expectation, yet I could see that if I went back to teaching I would be isolated from my contemporaries.

After a few months we looked for more permanent accommodation and moved into a wonderful old weatherboard house perched high on Melton Hill overlooking Cleveland Bay. We had the front flat with expansive views of the islands – Magnetic, the Palm group and Hinchinbrook in the distance. The walls of the large enclosed veranda living area had been painted a dreadful shade of pink so we decided to repaint them white. We imagined this shade would better frame the picture-postcard scene of blue sea and tropical greenery. However, we seriously underestimated the effort it would take to fully cover the tongue and groove walls, high ceilings and wooden window louvres. It was February when we began this task and the heat and humidity almost defeated us, but eventually our exertions were rewarded as we completed the redecoration with purple and gold hessian curtains and seagrass matting.

At the beginning of 1966 I started teaching on a part-time basis at Cootharinga, a home run by the North Queensland Society for Crippled Children. This institution was quite familiar, reminding me of teaching at Devonfield and Lachlan Park in Tasmania, although there was much more focus on the physical care of severely disabled children and I relied more on nursing and therapy staff to assist me. I was appointed to develop a special program for those children who were multiply handicapped, because they did not qualify to attend the class run by the Education Department in another section of the institution. Two children were deaf and blind and several had complex physical and intellectual disabilities. Most children in my special group were residents because their families lived in isolated areas of North Queensland and they required full-time nursing care.

It was at Cootharinga that I first met and worked with Aboriginal children, but I found it very difficult to gain their confidence and their physical and sensory disabilities limited my choice of educational methods. I found that music and art were particularly popular, especially when I sang nonsense rhymes while I supervised physical exercises. These children suffered from the same kind of isolation and deprivation as the children I had taught in Tasmania a few years earlier. The restrictive attitudes to disability prevailed in both the medical and the education professions. There was a double disadvantage for institutionalised Aboriginal children because they had been removed from their families and communities to be cared for by strangers. While the home was very well designed and attractive, the hospital environment restricted the children's emotional and intellectual response. There was little understanding of Aborigines and certainly no recognition of their culture. In class most youngsters were apparently unable to articulate their thoughts and needs. I started to notice the impact of cultural difference on these children's educational experience.

While I was teaching at Cootharinga Henry and I shared the responsibility of caring for John. I went off to school each morning, returning home at lunchtime to take over from Henry, who then worked at the university until evening. However, as both our jobs became more demanding we had on occasions to find alternative child care. One of the few centres available was on the top floor of the grand old Townsville City Council building with attractive iron lacework around its verandas. As a lively toddler John was very happy to spend some time there playing with other children. It was a casual childcare facility primarily for women to leave their children while shopping, but it was a good backup arrangement for us.

One day I arrived to collect John and discovered the childcare centre strangely silent. I knocked loudly at the entrance and eventually a solitary staff member emerged to apologise and announce that all the children were next door completing fire drill. I was rather surprised but was invited in to watch the final stages of this exercise. Standing by a large open window I watched two women leaning out to receive a small child who was being carefully passed across the narrow gap between the buildings. The fire drill actually involved children being evacuated from the top floor of the old wooden building to the safety of the brick building next door. Male bank staff in the adjoining building obviously took this fire safety routine very seriously and no one except me seemed at all perturbed by this risky process. However, had a child suddenly panicked or an adult lost their grip the consequences of a fall would have been fatal. I was aghast that John had already been part of this regular exercise, but he was cheerfully watching the other children's return and was of course oblivious to my anxiety. In retrospect I can but admire the ingenuity and commitment of all those involved. At least staff had recognised that the building was indeed a potential firetrap and planned an escape route. Nevertheless it is indeed a salutary reminder of the era, when there were no formal standards of child care. After this experience we found alternative child care with a neighbour who ran a playgroup in her home.

In that first year in Townsville our social life mainly revolved around visiting friends or inviting them home to our flat for a meal, but one day Henry suggested we go out for dinner at a local hotel the following week. My initial enthusiasm waned when I realised our rare night out involved attending an Australian Labor Party (ALP) fundraising dinner in honour of Arthur Calwell, then Federal Opposition Leader. I had thought we were going to a restaurant and an evening with an earnest guest speaker seemed a pretty poor alternative.

It was a typical sultry night so I chose the only 'special' item in my wardrobe – a very short, brown and white mini dress I had bought in London. Henry was dressed casually too, so we were embarrassed to see that everyone else was formally attired, the men in dark, double-breasted suits that defied logic in the humid climate of the tropics. The women were more at ease in colourful, loose-fitting dresses, but my brief skirt and bare legs were very much out of place for such a formal occasion. It seemed that only 'elderly' people were prepared to spend a Saturday evening with Mr Calwell. Several glances in our direction were quite disapproving and one trade unionist asked me why we were there when Henry was at the university. It seemed a strange question, but at this time the local union movement had no experience of a young middle-class academic getting involved in the ALP.

I sat surrounded by people I didn't know, wishing the evening would pass quickly. I remember watching the shambling figure of Arthur Calwell coming to speak at the lectern, which had an Australian flag draped across the front. Mr Calwell's opening remarks and style of presentation were scarcely riveting and I felt my Saturday night was definitely doomed. But suddenly this old man was talking about the Vietnam War and strongly arguing against the conscription of young Australians. I became focused on this speech, listening intently to his arguments and the questions that were to follow. I wrote about that evening in a letter to my mother, saying: 'I met Mr Calwell on Saturday – I think he is genuinely concerned about what is happening to the Vietnamese people and doesn't want Australians to be involved in the war but it seems unfair he is rarely reported in a good light'.

At the time, I had very little interest in party politics and family legend records that on the night of the 1966 election I was ironing in the kitchen, interrupting Henry's monitoring of results now and then to ask, 'How's it going now, dear?'

I have often said it was the Vietnam War which actually politicised me because I *was* concerned about conscription and was genuinely surprised that a government could so easily introduce a policy that selected young men at random to go into military service and be sent to a war zone. I could well imagine my own distress if our son were ever to be conscripted in the future. Soon after that meeting with Arthur Calwell, I embarked on my first political campaign in Townsville by starting a branch of 'Save Our Sons'. This was an anti-conscription organisation established by women opposed to the compulsory ballot of nineteen-year-old boys who could then be sent to fight in the Vietnam War. I had read about 'Save Our Sons' being launched in Melbourne and Sydney, so decided Townsville needed to be part of what was to become a national anti-conscription campaign. This small initiative was to set the direction of my future political career and my commitment to the peace movement.

Just a few women came to the first meeting I held at our home on Melton Hill. Most were women with teenage sons at risk of the Federal Government's conscription policy and they were much more knowledgeable about this issue than me. I met Loma Thompson and Esme Hardy who became important mentors, teaching me how to be effective in a Townsville community organisation. I had no knowledge of the local scene and was just starting to develop an understanding of the Vietnam War and the Australian Government's role in introducing conscription.

Henry and I had already joined the Townsville Peace Committee where we met Senator Jim Keeffe, then National President of the Australian Labor Party, and leading trade unionists Fred Thompson, North Queensland Organiser for the Amalgamated Metal Workers' Union, and Bill Irvine, local secretary of the Australian Meat Workers' Union. Initially I was somewhat intimidated by these older men, who seemed to have such a broad understanding of the political issues of the day. There were only a few women involved at the time and the men dominated the discussion, but I listened and started to take an interest in political debate, especially where it related to conscription.

My initiative in establishing a branch of 'Save Our Sons' in Townsville was welcomed by the Townsville Peace Committee and attracted considerable local media attention. In an article headed 'Wants to Form Branch of SOS', the *Townsville Daily Bulletin* reported:

> A young Townsville woman who opposes conscription of youth for service in Vietnam has decided to do something to fight what she considers is abhorrent. The objective of the 'Save Our Sons' movement shall be to seek the amendment or repeal of the

> present National Service Act, particularly with regard to objectionable clauses providing for long periods of compulsory service, engagement in military action abroad and severe penalties for infringements.

The article, describing me as a part-time housewife and schoolteacher, focused on the fact that I was 'too young to have a son eligible for conscription', but did include the quote I had read in a news report about a prominent Victorian anti-war activist, Jean McLean: 'We regard our activities as acts of patriotism in the interest of peace and life for Australians and for people around the world'.

Overnight I became the subject of media interest, with the local television station wanting images of mother and infant son. The publicity surrounding my involvement in an anti-Vietnam War campaign attracted criticism even from people we regarded as friends and colleagues. One woman told me she could no longer continue our friendship as her priest had warned her not to associate with communists. I was too amazed to be upset by her revelation and had to check with Henry precisely why such an allegation had been made.

One media outlet went so far as to report that the wife of university lecturer, Henry Reynolds, had established a branch of 'Save Our Sons'. Several staff members were horrified that this young upstart was responsible for bringing discredit to the university's good name. A friend reported that it had been suggested that 'Reynolds should control his wife'. This belief that men took responsibility for 'managing' their wives was not uncommon in the 1960s and in the very macho environment of North Queensland it was assumed that Henry should have been able to prevent his wife from embarrassing him.

I learned a great deal about politics in that first year in

Townsville. I began to identify key politicians and listen to their interviews on radio and television. I was better able to follow government processes and learn how people could lobby to change policy by appealing to public opinion. I also became familiar with the way the local media could be used as my friend Shirley Gilliver – herself a broadcaster – taught me how to write press releases and condense information for radio and television interviews. It was much more difficult to gain support from the media than it had been when I was working for recognition of intellectually disabled children.

When yet another of my 'Save Our Sons' press releases had been ignored, Shirley advised me to turn it into a letter to the editor, because it might have more chance of being printed. I decided to present it personally as we knew the editor was a strong supporter of Australia's involvement in the Vietnam War. I dressed very carefully for the meeting, tying back my long hair and choosing a more traditional skirt and blouse so that I looked the part of a respectable young mother. I was shown into the editor's office and found myself confronted by a large, florid-faced gentleman smoking behind a chaotic desk. He glared at me and left me standing to hesitantly present myself. I managed to stutter a few words and hand over my carefully typed letter. He glanced at my words, grunted dismissively and shouted, 'You know what I think of this!' and ripped the letter up in front of me. He then returned to his work, ignoring me as I tried to leave with some remnants of dignity.

I was angry about his level of control in this situation but had no idea how to respond. I left his office and hurried back to tell my friend about the way I had been treated. While she sympathised with me, Shirley also reminded me that I should not be surprised that my anti–Vietnam War stance was unpopular. Yet I expected people to listen to alternative opinions and it seemed wrong that an editor could simply refuse to print a letter that had been drafted to present another side of the argument.

This incident only made me more determined to continue my efforts to change attitudes and to challenge the prevailing views in Townsville's generally pro-military community. After the initial shock value of 'Save Our Sons' being established in Townsville, it became harder to attract media attention. I thought of a new strategy to get people involved by conducting street opinion polls. Of course they were not professionally designed but I thought I knew the questions we needed to ask about Australia's involvement in Vietnam. Armed with clipboards, several members of SOS took it in turns to walk up and down Flinders Street asking strangers whether Australian boys should be conscripted and sent to war. The response to my initiative was unexpected – a surprising number of people were prepared to record their opposition. However, opinion was deeply divided, so SOS members were often subjected to hostile abuse from those who strongly defended government policy. One man reported us to the police and a young officer was promptly dispatched to order us off the street.

I complained about this treatment to our new friends at the Townsville Trades and Labour Council, the headquarters of the Townsville Peace Committee. Fred Thompson patiently explained the process of obtaining a police permit to conduct such activity in a public place, so I went to the local police station to apply for official permission. I was kept waiting while my unusual request was checked out by somewhat suspicious police officers. Finally, a kindly senior sergeant came to the counter and gently suggested I reconsider my request, as the matter would take time because the paperwork would have to go to Brisbane. My distinct impression was that he sympathised with what I wanted to do because he confided to me that his son had just turned nineteen and his family was very uneasy about the next ballot. It was an unexpected response but he obviously knew that the application was unlikely to be approved.

The application was duly submitted but I never received a response, so SOS was not able to officially continue our street polling efforts. Instead we kept questionnaires in our handbags and approached anyone we knew – even vaguely – urging them to quickly respond to our surreptitious questioning. We hoped this resembled a normal footpath conversation between friends, but it was not very successful and eventually we abandoned the strategy. However, I was able to use some of the information for press releases and I managed to get several radio interviews in which I reported that Townsville people were just as divided in public opinion about Australia's involvement in the Vietnam War as people in capital cities.

Of course it was a claim I could not validate because our polling methods were so amateurish but I was convinced of the merit of my argument, ignoring sceptical journalists who pointed out that Townsville people were more likely to be proud of their association with the Vietnam War because the city hosted a large military base. The Townsville Peace Committee welcomed the publicity I was able to generate and I was asked to help put together a short report to give Prime Minister Harold Holt when he visited Townsville. A young clergyman, John Beer, and I were asked to make the presentation and somehow we were able to find out that the prime minister's party was staying at a motel on the beachfront.

Looking back from today's security conscious environment, it seems quite extraordinary that we were able to go to the front office and ask precisely which units were booked in the prime minister's name. I may have been a fresh-faced youngster but the lack of official security and scrutiny seems unbelievable forty years on. Yet on that occasion I was given the number of 'Mr Holt's' unit and could have knocked on that door, but wisely chose the door to the right where a member of staff was located. A senior adviser came to the door in pyjamas and was surprisingly affable about our unannounced presence and suggested we wait while he checked to see if the prime minister was awake. Several minutes later Harold Holt, in a tweed dressing gown, appeared to shake our hands and accept our protest. We were both very impressed with the informality of this friendly response. I presume there must have been Federal Police officers on duty nearby but any casual observer would have seen just an older man enjoying the early morning sun as he had a brief exchange with his two young visitors.

I cannot really explain my determination to be so involved in this level of activism at this time. I was pregnant with our second child, Anna, and had plenty to do teaching part time, managing our new home and caring for two-year-old John. Despite my teaching experience in Tasmania and London I was still quite tentative about confronting authority, yet Townsville provided the kind of environment where I thought 'someone should do something' and it seemed I was the person available.

I have always regarded my fledgling efforts in 'Save Our Sons' as a significant contributing factor in my 'coming of age' as a community activist. My political awareness was heightened by the experience of working on this issue because it gave me insights at local, national and international levels. At no time would I have boasted that my somewhat ad hoc approach to advocacy in Townsville had made much impact. However, it certainly influenced my development as I established my own identity in a community that defined a woman by her husband's career. I became more confident about my own opinions and about taking a stand on principle. This period was also important in showing me I could combine my roles as wife and mother with being involved in the community. I discovered it was possible to take John to meetings and to juggle phone interviews with the sound of childish prattle in the background.

Many years later in the 1990s history lecturer Dawn May asked me to give a guest lecture on the Vietnam War to students at the Cairns Campus of James Cook University. During my presentation I noticed a mature-aged male student taking copious notes and nodding in agreement with some of my comments. After the lecture he came up to me and said, 'I have watched you for a very long time and I want to shake your hand and say congratulations'. I assumed that this was indeed a friendly and supportive constituent who was being particularly complimentary about my parliamentary career, so I thanked him and moved on to talk with other students. He remained in the group until almost everyone else had left, when he said he wanted to tell me something very important about the Australian Vietnam protest movement. He announced that as a young ASIO officer he had been sent to Townsville to monitor the activities of 'Save Our Sons', and confessed to having followed me on several occasions. Naturally I was very sceptical about this possibility and initially treated it as a joke but as the conversation developed I realised he was quite serious. His lecturer later confirmed that this student had indeed worked in ASIO and that he was unlikely to invent such a story.

No doubt I could attempt to verify his claim by researching ASIO files to see if there is any record of such scrutiny. Nevertheless, it remains a tantalising reminder of the attitude towards people working in the Australian peace movement in the 1960s.

CHAPTER 5

Confronting racism 1965–1969

THE MOST CONFRONTING aspect of life in North Queensland was the racism. It permeated the atmosphere with the same intensity as the tropical sun. When I knew we were moving to North Australia, I had announced: 'I would like to help the Aborigines up there'. I cannot recall what prompted this somewhat patronising intention except that living in London had made me very aware of different cultures. I knew very little about Australian Aborigines and certainly had no knowledge of their history or culture.

My first personal experience of racism occurred within the early months of adjusting to life on the northern frontier. I was pushing John's pram along Flinders Street past a number of already rowdy hotel bars. Suddenly a body was hurled from a hotel and it landed with a sickening thud right in front of us. A young Aboriginal man lay apparently unconscious on the pavement as John pointed and said, 'Look poor man'. I was momentarily transfixed by this appalling sight of the stranger lying in a pool of blood, but recovered sufficiently to run into the closest hotel for help. My demand for someone to phone an ambulance resulted in a chorus of laughter and wolf whistles. The barman ordered me out of this exclusively masculine domain, reminding me that 'No bloody sheilas are allowed in here!'

Returning to the footpath, I negotiated the pram around the slumped body and ran towards the nearest phone, which was in the next block at the Post Office. The response from the ambulance officer was even more shocking than at the hotel. He asked my name and address, my relationship to the injured person, whether he had ambulance membership coverage, was he drunk and, finally, was he *only* an Aborigine? In desperation, I rang the police.

Despite the reputation of the Queensland Police in the 1960s, on this occasion my call was answered promptly and I was assured that a patrol car would be sent immediately. I was not happy about my final decision, convinced that the price of medical attention was probably a charge for being 'drunk and disorderly'. I rang back later, determined to put on record the gross negligence of hotel and ambulance staff. The duty officer dismissed my enquiry saying, 'Look here, lady, we don't keep records of all the blacks we have to pick up around town'.

I was disturbed by this incident. The memory of those drinkers' derisive laughter lingered as I tried to explain to myself why I had been so powerless to get appropriate help. At first, it was hard to believe that there was such open hostility to an Aboriginal person needing medical attention – and why had he been thrown so brutally from a public bar? In this town, Aborigines were regarded as second-class citizens who had no right to expect the same standards as white people. I heard the complaints mouthed by taxi drivers and shopkeepers who loudly condemned the government for 'allowing those bloody boongs into town'. The aggression in their voices overwhelmed rational debate and explained a great deal about the attitudes of people towards Aborigines. It also gave me an appreciation of why Aboriginal families responded to overtures of friendship with such distrust and suspicion. I now understood why many would studiously avoid eye contact and kept their distance. Aboriginal women I saw in playgrounds were reluctant to engage in the kind of casual conversation mothers share when supervising their children.

In 1966 I read an advertisement in the local paper announcing the annual general meeting of the One People of Australia League (OPAL), an organisation concerned with Aboriginal welfare. When I went along I met just a few elderly people who were struggling to maintain a Townsville branch. There was only one other young person, a most attractive woman with dark skin who introduced herself as Roberta Sykes, but cheerfully announced 'Everyone calls me Bobbi'. She told the meeting she had grown up in Townsville and had lived with the local racism her colour attracted. Bobbi and I were welcomed with much enthusiasm to OPAL; I was asked to take on the position of secretary and Bobbi became treasurer. We had no idea of the origins or focus of this organisation because communication with the Brisbane headquarters was minimal and we just focused on what we saw as the importance of tackling racism in Townsville.

At this time both Bobbi and I became increasingly aware of the civil rights movement in the United States, where 'Black Power' campaigners attracted international headlines. We knew about the efforts of Aboriginal activist Charles Perkins, who had led a 'Freedom Ride' through country New South Wales to identify discrimination in country towns, where Aborigines were segregated in picture theatres and unable to swim in council swimming pools. We wanted to bring these debates to North Queensland, but we later learned that OPAL Brisbane had a much more cautious approach to the wellbeing of Aborigines. Nevertheless the Townsville branch wanted to work with their energetic young members, so we started to set a new direction.

Bobbi and I took on our new responsibilities with a crusading zeal and became firm friends in the process. We worked at each other's kitchen tables planning fresh avenues for promoting Aboriginal issues. We also met for lunch and I learnt from harsh experience that my new friend faced a colour bar in most hotels and coffee shops and, on occasions, we were both asked to leave certain premises. There seemed no avenue for complaint and these very unpleasant incidents reinforced my impressions of racism and segregation in this city.

Later that year, Bobbi and I were sent as Townsville delegates to the state conference of OPAL in Brisbane and it was here we discovered that the Queensland Government was very much in control of our organisation. There were few young people at this carefully stage-managed event, but Bobbi and I immediately identified with the well-articulated advocacy of Pat O'Shane, Mick Miller and John Newfong who were there from other branches in Queensland. Like Bobbi, these young people later became very well known Aboriginal activists working for Indigenous rights in the 1970s and 1980s. Bobbi was Australia's first Harvard graduate and Pat O'Shane achieved national prominence as an outspoken magistrate and human rights campaigner. Most delegates at the conference were well-meaning Queenslanders wanting to help improve conditions for Aborigines, but the atmosphere reeked of white middle-class paternalism and was not receptive to the ideas of my new friends.

On the second day of the conference, one speaker presented a particularly vicious diatribe against 'communist agitators befriending our poor Aboriginal brothers', ranting at great length against such associations. Bobbi and I exchanged glances, as we both knew several Communist Party members in Townsville. At the end of this speech, Bobbi bravely joined the few questioners to ask about state government policy on housing Aboriginal families. The speaker was in fact Pat Killoran, the powerful Director of the Department of Native Affairs. He was much feared in the Aboriginal community, not just because he set the direction of government policy but also because he had absolute power over the lives of Aborigines. He gave Bobbi a dismissive glance and proceeded to lecture her about the dangers of meddling in matters she did not understand. I was enraged by his condescension and somehow got to my feet to demand a proper answer to her very legitimate question. I too was unsuccessful in gaining any useful response, but Bobbi and I shared some satisfaction in confronting the man with the tyrannical reputation.

I was surprised by the intensity of my challenge to this figure of authority. It was another turning point – asserting myself in a world that still expected young women to meekly accept the word of men in power. No doubt it was at this conference that Bobbi and I raised doubts in the minds of OPAL Brisbane members about the direction of its Townsville branch. However, communication was limited between the head office and its branches so we returned north to continue working in ways that certainly would not have gained the approval of the Director of Native Affairs.

In August 1966 the Gurindji Aboriginal stockmen went on strike. They walked off a pastoral station at Wave Hill in the Northern Territory in protest against their low wages and inadequate living conditions. Bobbi and I read about this landmark event – the first stance in Australian Aborigines' land rights struggle – and sent a telegram of support. We then persuaded our local committee to donate money from OPAL's meagre funds to assist the Gurindji leader, Vincent Lingiari, who had established a camp for workers and their families at Wattie Creek. Through our contacts with the Trades and Labour Council we had the opportunity to meet two Gurindji members when they came to Townsville as part of a national public awareness strategy.

That year OPAL wanted to organise a special occasion to mark National Aborigines and Islanders Day, so it became my responsibility to plan a Townsville event on the day. Because of my experiences as a teacher, I decided on an art competition and exhibition to give Aboriginal children the opportunity to show their work. I visited a number of schools that had substantial enrolments of Indigenous children. At one school I was ushered into the headmaster's office, where a genial man in his forties seemed very helpful and interested in this project. He arranged for me to speak to each class and agreed to the school being a collection point for entries. As I was about to leave, he told me it was a good idea to promote art and sport among Aboriginal children and confided: 'Of course they will never achieve anything academically, you know – as their brains are smaller than ours'.

This highly offensive statement was typical of the attitudes which so influenced the direction of Queensland's education policy in the 1960s. I was especially shocked that such a statement could be made by a headmaster who seemed to have no particular malice towards Aborigines, yet his prejudice obviously affected his expectations of these pupils. Within the Queensland Education Department there was no acknowledgement of Aboriginal culture, language or learning style. Indigenous children were expected to adapt to the rigid Anglo-centric curriculum.

This led me to set up a kindergarten for 'disadvantaged' children, the majority of whom were Aborigines and Torres Strait Islanders. It was towards the end of 1966 and I was leaving Cootharinga because our second child, Anna, was due in April the following year. I had read about 'Operation Headstart' – a compensatory educational program for preschool children that was trying to reach out to Afro-American and other poor children living in the slums of American cities. My teaching in London's East End and at Cootharinga had alerted me to some of the educational issues for children who spoke another language or who came from a different cultural background. I wanted to try to provide some kind of bridge between home and school, so that the culture shock of Queensland's education system would be lessened. I knew early childhood education was important for children developing their language and pre-reading skills. Yet many Aboriginal children did not speak 'standard' English and those from the Torres Strait were learning English as their second language. Furthermore, the general attitudes to Aborigines were either paternalistic or dismissive, so it seemed to me children needed some preparation to manage their introduction to formal education.

I was especially committed to the kindergarten, as it combined my own professional background with the new social environment in which we lived. I talked to Aboriginal and Torres Strait Islander families I knew and visited families I had never met, earnestly outlining the benefits of the kindergarten. My local OPAL committee enthusiastically accepted the idea and the Presbyterian Church offered the use of their central hall in Stokes Street for three mornings a week. I began collecting toys and basic equipment, just as I had done for special schools in Tasmania. However, I found it much more difficult to raise support for this idea. Clearly the sympathy for disabled children did not extend to children of another culture.

Nevertheless a number of friends helped me open the OPAL Kindergarten for three and four year olds in January 1967. We relied on volunteers to drive the children to and from the city because families were scattered across different suburbs and public transport was limited. I organised the rosters and helped supervise the program of preschool activities. I wanted to ensure the program was up and running before Anna's birth. In the early weeks only a few children attended because there was some uncertainty among families about the idea. At the time I could not understand why Aboriginal families were initially reluctant to have their children driven off by strangers. I did make every effort to encourage mothers to accompany their children, but for those with babies and younger children this was not usually possible.

Henry and I had met Eddie and Bonita Mabo socially so they were among the first parents to show trust in the kindergarten and this gave other families the confidence to allow their children to attend. I did not drive at the time so I depended on Henry to drive me around to collect groups of children. One day when Anna's arrival was imminent he went alone to collect the children but found that a white man's arrival at an Aboriginal home caused consternation as the children ran to hide and parents peered anxiously from windows. On this occasion, just one child did not run away and Henry described his experience in the introduction to his first book, *The Other Side of the Frontier*:

> One day a little girl of four or five did not run away. She stood in the middle of the path and stared at me in silence. She looked at me, not as an individual or as a male or a well-meaning academic, but as a white man, a 'migloo' with a fear that was not personal at all, but historical, communal and unforgettable.

It was many years before we really understood the legacy of the Stolen Generation and could understand how foolish and arrogant it had been for me to assume that I could sweep into Aborigines' and Torres Strait Islanders' lives to organise their 'education'. Viewed today, in a very different era, I can appreciate that my zealous efforts 'to help the Aborigines' reflected the assimilation policies promoted at the time. Yet there was a need for some new ideas and sensitive partnerships which could start to counter the extremes of racism and neglect.

Working with Aboriginal and Torres Strait Islander children at the kindergarten was a challenge for me as a special educator. On the one hand, their enthusiasm for play and many activities was very familiar, yet I found it difficult to engage them in more traditional pre-reading activities. I knew the theory of 'readiness' for formal learning and did not want to be overly prescriptive, but I wanted to give some practical assistance in that final year before children met the very demanding expectations of Queensland's Grade 1 curriculum. I searched the library for books of interest to children whose cultural background and experience was not reflected in most standard texts. Action stories and games enabled us to build on the language skills which were so important for Aboriginal and Torres Strait Islander children to acquire before starting school.

Anna Marie Reynolds was born at the Townsville General Hospital on 15 April 1967. Her birth was very straightforward except that she arrived at the end of a morning shift and I found myself left on the delivery table within sight of my new baby, lying on a bench nearby. I was cold and thirsty. I remembered the nurses who had fussed around me after John was born and I longed for a hot drink. I waited and waited for sounds of staff on the new shift coming to find us. I looked for a bell but finally gave up and gingerly eased myself into a standing position. I shuffled my way around to Anna and paused to admire her. She was lying quietly but I was worried she too would be feeling the extreme effects of the air conditioning so I picked her up and walked slowly out the door. I must have been a strange sight still in my hospital gown clutching an unwashed newborn infant wrapped in a towel. I got as far as the lift where two young nurses emerged, horrified that I was on my feet. They rushed around, put me in a wheelchair and took Anna off to the nursery. I was duly showered and helped into bed, where I was instructed to remain for at least three days.

Anna was a model baby and after a few days we went home. I settled in to a very pleasant household routine of caring for two children while continuing my voluntary work with 'Save our Sons' and OPAL. Three mornings a week I taught at the kindergarten where John played and Anna slept. I did not experience any of the anxieties I had in London because life in the tropics made everything so much easier. I didn't have to worry about the effect of winter temperatures and the washing dried in a few hours. I had learned to relax and enjoy my role as a mother while still getting on with work that interested me.

OPAL was very involved in promoting the 'yes' case for the national referendum to be held on 27 May 1967, when Australian voters were asked to decide whether two specific sections of the Australian Constitution should be amended. One question related to the Federal Government being able to take responsibility for Aboriginal policy and the second enabled Aborigines to be included in the National Census for data collection purposes. Both reforms were especially important to the wellbeing of Queensland Aborigines, who had suffered such discrimination under the repressive state legislation of successive administrations. On polling day I left the children with Henry and spent a couple of hours handing out 'Vote Yes' leaflets. Most people made no comment but several people's abusive reaction clearly reflected the strength of the 'no' vote. While there was an overwhelming majority nationally in favour of reforming the Constitution to benefit Aborigines, the negative vote was greater in country regions. In Queensland the coastal towns gave slightly less support than the national average of 89 per cent, but there was a significantly lower 'yes' vote in western and remote communities, where people were used to assuming Aborigines did not need any special recognition.

After the success of the May 1967 referendum the Townsville Trades and Labour Council initiated the idea of a major seminar about the implications of that decision. I was invited to represent OPAL Townsville at the first community meeting at the Townsville City Council, at which representatives of the university, city council, churches, community organisations and the Townsville Trades and Labour Council agreed to establish the Inter-Racial Citizens Committee. I was asked to become secretary and began organising the two-day event to be held in December that year. We called it: 'We the Australians: What is to follow the Referendum?'

Keynote speakers Faith Bandler (NSW) and Joe McGinnes (Qld) from the Federal Council for the Advancement of Aboriginal and Torres Strait Islanders together with well-known academics, Professor Charles Rowley and Dr Colin Tatz, confirmed their attendance, which was a tremendous boost for the local committee.

The committee met regularly at the Townsville City Council to plan every detail of this landmark event. However, after a couple of months several committee members reported strange happenings that seemed to be linked to their membership of the Inter-Racial Citizens Committee. One member was asked by his employer to resign from the committee and another was told by his priest that this seminar would be 'taken over by communists'. Another was sure he was being followed home after a particular meeting. At about the same time I received a letter from the State Secretary of OPAL indicating that the Townsville branch should withdraw its membership of the Inter-Racial Citizens Committee. In due course we were advised further that OPAL was not to be associated with the forthcoming event. A statement from a member of the OPAL Board of Directors was published locally stating: 'the seminar was against the aims of OPAL which stipulated that the organisation was non-political and non-sectarian'.

OPAL Townsville, led by Anglican clergyman John Clarkson, initially refused to comply, arguing that the directive was both arbitrary and unreasonable. However, when he checked our legal status he found that under OPAL's constitution our local branch was obliged to act. The Townsville branch of OPAL ceased to function because the only active members left wanted to keep working with the Inter-Racial Citizens Committee and at the kindergarten, which we renamed Kindergarten Headstart.

However, OPAL's opposition was not the only sign that the seminar was attracting criticism. In organising this event we relied on donations and the goodwill of local businesses. It was my job to keep the records of names of people making donations as several individuals and businesses had committed to being official sponsors. One Sunday morning I spent a couple of hours reviewing the correspondence and recording the donations, which had been made so that a number of cheques were ready to be banked the following day. In the afternoon Henry and I took the children for a walk down to the beach near Anzac Park leaving our flat unlocked, as was the custom in the relaxed environment of Townsville at this time. When we returned, all my papers were scattered over the floor and at first I assumed the sea breeze was responsible. However, on closer examination, I found that the cheques and a list of names were missing. Naturally I was very concerned and wondered if we had been burgled. But cash and other items in the flat had not been touched. I phoned several committee members, who advised me to report the 'burglary' to the police. I went to the police station to make my complaint and it was clear that the police officer on duty thought my story lacked credibility.

After all, who would bother to steal a few cheques and a list of names? Within a few days the cheques were 'found' by police, who handed them over to the Trades and Labour Council, but my detailed list of names, addresses and phone numbers was never located. A neighbour reported seeing two men in a parked van outside our home not long after we had left that particular afternoon. The fact that a similar van was reported following several Inter-Racial Citizens Committee members after meetings could never be verified. However, we were able to confirm Queensland Special Branch surveillance of the seminar itself. We observed two cars with plain clothes officers parked in the blazing December sun for the entire first day – apparently recording the number plates of every car entering the Pimlico Campus of the university.

Despite all the controversy in the lead-up to 'We the Australians: What is to follow the Referendum?' the event itself was a great success, attracting more than 300 participants. It generated considerable interest and for some Aborigines and Torres Strait Islanders the weekend became a turning point for their local activism. The Brisbane *Courier Mail*'s headline read 'Aboriginal laws similar to jail rules' and it was reported that prominent Aboriginal leader, Mr J McGinnes, had told the seminar in Townsville that 'Queensland laws for Aboriginal and Torres Strait Islanders were similar to regulations controlling prisons and mental hospitals'.

Furthermore, he said the Queensland legislation relating to Aborigines was ' . . . sheer mockery of the idea that Aboriginal missions should be modern self-governing communities'.

On the Monday morning after the weekend seminar I went as usual to Kindergarten Headstart. The children arrived just after 9 am but my two regular volunteers were unable to come that day, so I wondered how to occupy fifteen youngsters on such a hot morning. It was slightly cooler outside so I set up a range of outdoor activities but then noticed a car with four men parked opposite. I could not believe that the kindergarten was being monitored in the same way that the weekend seminar had been. Initially I was very uneasy, especially as I was on my own that morning, but then thought the situation was quite ludicrous. The car remained in exactly the same position until lunchtime, with the burly plain clothes officers making several trips to a nearby shop for cool drinks. They did not leave until all the children were collected to go home. It seemed that members of Special Branch had been instructed to record the number plates of anyone associated with Kindergarten Headstart. Such police operations may seem unlikely to many people today, but they reflected the level of official paranoia about anyone promoting new opportunities for Queensland Aborigines and Torres Strait Islanders, when the most benign activity was viewed with suspicion.

I found that weekend seminar very challenging as it was the first time that I had participated in discussion which seriously addressed the racism I knew was deeply embedded in North Queensland. It was in a sense almost reassuring to have the two-day debate confirm the doubts and fears I had of my own society.

The seminar formally endorsed the significant role of Kindergarten Headstart in providing more culturally appropriate preschool experiences, so we began planning for a more professional approach. This led to the eventual appointment of a trained kindergarten teacher and a major community appeal for funds, which guaranteed its future. Parents took on the work of the management committee and several years later Kindergarten Headstart received official recognition from both State and Federal Governments. The purpose-built kindergarten in Currajong has now successfully provided early childhood education to hundreds of Indigenous children for forty years.

In 1968 I helped to organise 'homework classes' for Indigenous students at one of the local schools, where volunteers assisted children with homework and extra coaching. While this again was a program based on volunteers, its concept originated from ABSCHOL (the Aboriginal Scholarship Scheme). ABSCHOL was an initiative of the Australian Union of Students, aimed at financially supporting Aboriginal students to further their secondary education and enter tertiary institutions.

That year I attended an ABSCHOL conference in Sydney, where teachers from around Australia and New Zealand focused on practical initiatives in teaching Aboriginal children as well as research into the impact of cultural factors in learning. Queensland was the only state that did not send an Education Department representative because it did not believe in identifying special programs for Aboriginal and Islander children. I returned north reinvigorated and reassured that my preliminary efforts in Aboriginal education were moving in the right direction. I was also able to hand over a $400 scholarship fund for Townsville High School students – a worthwhile addition to our work in running the homework classes.

I also became involved in campaigning against discrimination in employment. When a national company opened its major store in November 1968 Henry and I arranged to bring at least thirty Aboriginal and Islander women into the city for interviews. All were interviewed and asked the standard questions for jobs in the new shop and cafeteria, but not one was employed. I sought an interview with the Northern Division Supervisor who was overseeing a five million dollar development of stores in Townsville, Cairns and Mt Isa. He refused to explain the failure of his company to employ Aboriginal or Torres Strait Islander women, saying only that it was company policy to employ 'on merit'. My friend Shirley interviewed me on radio and asked me directly if the company was actually discriminating against employing any one from the large group. I not only confirmed that this was my view of the situation but I urged Aborigines and Islanders to boycott the new store. Our friend Bob Greenwood, a local lawyer, warned me that I risked possible legal action, so I did not repeat this call. Everyone was very excited about the opening of such a large, attractive shopping complex so it is doubtful that anyone took my call seriously. Yet it was many years before Townsville businesses employed Indigenous people in city stores.

During those early years in Townsville Henry and I came face to face with the reality of indigenous people's lives in North Queensland. We met so many of the local elders who just wanted life to be better for their children and grandchildren. There were wonderful individuals like Daisy Duffin, Eva Geia, Jack Barry, Monty Pryor, Bonita and Eddie Mabo who introduced us to their history and culture, patiently explaining the way they had been forced to hide their language and stories. Their quiet dignity in recounting the terrible injustices they had suffered was very influential in directing Henry's academic research and my activism.

Daisy was from Mona Mona, an Aboriginal reserve in the rainforest behind Cairns. She cared for her two grandsons after her daughter had died in childbirth. She came to see me for help in arranging to have the boys officially transferred to her care. She spoke sadly of Gloria's death a few months earlier, saying only that there was no doctor or access to hospital for the complicated labour. Her quiet acceptance that Gloria's young life could end so abruptly when any other Australian woman would have had the necessary medical care reflected the reality of Aboriginal women's experience. A committed Christian, Daisy did not seek to question or blame. Later she recounted stories of her life on the mission, where moralistic control separated boys and girls at puberty. She was removed from her family to live in the girls' dormitory. On one occasion, she was found talking to a boy so her head was shaved as punishment. The shame of that experience remained with her as she told her story at least twenty-five years later.

It was stories like these which helped us understand the history of racism and to start to identify ways in which we could contribute to changing attitudes and policies.

CHAPTER 6

Becoming a feminist 1969–1975

I RETURNED TO TEACHING full time in 1969, when I joined the Queensland Education Department and was appointed to Aitkenvale Primary School, then catering for children in a new suburb on the outskirts of Townsville. I had asked for a school where I could continue working with Aboriginal children but the local office assured me there was no apartheid in Queensland. I knew some of the cultural barriers these children faced but there was no official departmental recognition of such issues at this time.

On my first day back teaching I walked into a room crowded with old-fashioned wooden desks that were screwed to the floor, so there was limited scope for organising the seating of about forty children. I was familiar with more progressive environments in Tasmania and London, where there was the flexibility to move tables and chairs according to the activities involved. I was used to much more space and educational equipment, but my Queensland infant classroom offered just desks and a blackboard. Even the coloured chalk was rationed to a number of sticks per month.

Those early weeks were really difficult for me because I had not been trained to stand formally at a blackboard and drill six year olds in rote learning all day. I decided to introduce some changes that better suited this age group. First I had to create some space, so I persuaded two builders who were on site to remove one row of desks so that I had extra space in the classroom. They thought I just needed help to lift the furniture but were very good-humoured about having to spend some time using a crowbar to remove the heavily bolted desks. This row we relocated to the veranda outside my room so I could have outdoor activities. I was very pleased with the initial reorganisation and then began planning how to 'equip' the classroom.

John and Anna had a number of educational toys and many books so I persuaded them to lend them to my class. Each Sunday night they helped me pack a couple of boxes to transfer to school next morning and every Friday I restored them to their rightful owners. Of course I had to give John and Anna the opportunity to choose which favourite toys and books were exempt from this unofficial 'toy library', but they became quite enthusiastic about deciding what to lend each week. I bought rolls of butcher's paper and paints and scrounged through second-hand shops for mats and cushions. Soon my classroom was transformed into a much more colourful and comfortable place. The school's headmaster did not venture as far as the Infant Wing very often, but one day he appeared outside my room and stared with disbelief at the changes I had made. Fortunately my class was busily engaged in a variety of activities but I expected him to question my alternative approach to teaching. Instead he seemed quite impressed and within a short time I was asked to supervise student teachers and give demonstration lessons for the Townsville College of Advanced Education.

It was during this year that I began to experiment with

developing reading materials for Aboriginal and Islander children. The standard reading text used in infant classes throughout the state revolved around the lives of two English children named Dick and Dora. Their appearance and way of life was alien to most children living in tropical North Queensland, but they must have seemed very remote to Aboriginal children. I found it impossible to interest them in reading about these children's family life, which was so different from their own experience. It was Eddie Mabo's daughter Gail who taught me about culturally relevant reading material. She was obviously a very bright little girl who excelled at maths but was not motivated to read about Dick and Dora. One day she drew a magnificent picture of her family homeland, Murray Island, and I asked her to tell me about it. She talked enthusiastically, describing life on the island, and I wrote down the words and read them back to her. Each day we wrote more 'stories' about her family, which developed into her own reading book. Within a few months she could read many real-life stories she had illustrated and by the end of the year she was reading a range of books fluently. She had simply needed some familiar themes to approach written language that had relevance to her life experience. I continued using this approach with other indigenous children and found it made a significant difference in their early introduction to reading.

When I returned to the full-time work force I was completely unaware that my professional role as a teacher would be affected by being a married woman. Despite being well regarded as an innovative teacher I found that at the end of my first year my appointment was terminated. Initially I was shocked but the headmaster assured me this was quite normal and that, as a married woman, I would be reappointed to the same position the following year. I was not entitled to holiday pay and I discovered I was technically a 'temporary' teacher. I was indignant that my marital status had an impact on my professional role as a teacher and started to question the different way men and women were treated.

A particular personal experience led me to become involved in lobbying my local council about issues affecting women and children. I did not know much about feminism, but a domestic accident highlighted for me that women in the early 1970s were rarely taken seriously. It was Anna's birthday so I had taken several children to a local park and had just finished spreading out the food, drink and party hats on a colourful tablecloth in the shade of a large Moreton Bay fig tree. Suddenly there was a piercing scream and Anna came running from the playground, where she had cut her arm on a piece of unsecured swing chain. Her arm was bleeding profusely so I had to use the tablecloth as a temporary bandage and hurry a very dejected group of youngsters home for more appropriate first aid to be administered. When I realised the cut was only superficial the party was re-established at our kitchen table and, after we had all recovered from this unfortunate incident, I decided to report the faulty equipment to the Townsville City Council. I was unsure about areas of responsibility and the process of complaint, but was sufficiently motivated to phone and ask for the 'playground safety officer'. Of course there was no one answering to such a job description, but I finally spoke to a man from the Parks and Gardens Maintenance Section. I told my story, reporting the possibility of serious injury and demanding that the offending swing be repaired immediately.

I wanted a little sympathy and a promise of action, but in the 1970s the wheels of local government turned slowly and there was no apparent recognition of my complaint having any special urgency. I was told that playground equipment was repaired annually and I should lodge my complaint in writing. After the dramatic events of the afternoon I was in no mood for such a response so I told the council officer that he was guilty of ignoring children's safety. There was a pause while he digested this accusation from an obviously overwrought woman. 'There, there,' he said in a decidedly paternal tone, 'there's no need to get hysterical.'

Who could have predicted that this infuriatingly patronising response would help launch a political career in local and federal government? I not only lodged my complaint in writing, but also began talking to other women about the neglect of infrastructure and services for women and families in the northern city. We shared stories about being left behind because some local bus drivers would not allow folding prams aboard their buses. We commiserated with each other about the near-impossible task of negotiating laden prams around the fringes of busy streets, which had no ramped footpaths. There were few playgrounds, no designated school crossings and bikeways existed only in distant Europe. Traffic accidents involving children and teenagers occurred with alarming regularity, yet there was no obvious planning to avoid the increasing number of fatalities.

I drafted letters to the Townsville City Council stating the need for improved infrastructure and services that catered for women and families, but there was no response. Together with a few friends I decided to embark on a more strategic approach to find out just how decisions were made and how we could influence policy. Council meetings were held fortnightly in the late afternoon, an ideal time for avoiding scrutiny because in the early 1970s most men were at work and women at home preoccupied with tired children or hungry teenagers. It was agreed that we would try to roster two women to attend council meetings. When we attended we discovered the way that council worked through specific committees and we learned to record the names of councillors and staff responsible for our key areas of concern.

I was a regular visitor to the public gallery, but had to take John and Anna with me and try to concentrate while encouraging them to play at my feet during the meeting. Often they were surprisingly quiet because I brought along toys and a late afternoon snack to keep them happy. However, one day two bored youngsters constantly interrupted me and finally John used his best stage whisper to continually ask for a diverting trip to the toilet. It was a particularly tense moment in council debate so I continued writing in my notebook as his plaintive voice grew more demanding. Finally the Town Clerk left his place at the council table, strode to the public gallery area and said, 'Madam, let me take the boy to the gentlemen's convenience'.

Our presence seemed to encourage council to eventually transfer its meeting time to the evening, which made public attendance much easier. However, for more than twelve months our afternoon rosters enabled a number of local women to learn a great deal about the Townsville City Council and its policies. The only woman councillor, Joan Innes Reid, welcomed our support, admitting that the blatant sexism and bullying she experienced from most of her male colleagues was reduced by the presence of women in the public gallery. Nevertheless we were appalled by the behaviour of council members, who often indulged in aggressive tactics rather than focusing on the issue being considered. Two of us, Delma Benson and I, began to seriously consider the possibility of nominating for election to council ourselves.

In the meantime we began lobbying to have the Townsville City Council establish a Women's Advisory Committee. A comprehensive newspaper article reported our delegation's attendance at a general meeting with the headline 'Women's Committee Rebuffed by Council' and the article reported:

> The Mayor said, 'The council took the view that such a committee was not necessary. Women have no particular needs, which are inseparable from those of the rest of the community. Most of the things you ladies have talked about here tonight are social welfare needs and that is not the prerogative of local government.'
>
> In reply, Mrs Reynolds said she felt the city's public transport would improve quickly if council aldermen had to use this facility and she concluded, 'We are offering you our skills and special expertise.'

It was 1971 when I became directly involved in feminist debate. Women's liberation had reached Townsville and together with my friends I joined consciousness-raising evenings to discuss North American and European feminist movements and their implications for Australia. We read Betty Friedan, Simone de Beauvoir and Germaine Greer to discover the causes of women's oppression and to challenge the stereotypes of women and their limited role in society. I was particularly influenced by Eva Figes's *Patriarchal Attitudes* and readily identified with the young author pictured on the cover, which incorporated the subheading *My Case for Women to Revolt*. Her words inspired me. 'It's a man's world and to the extent that it is and remains a man's world it's going to remain a shabby deal for one half of humanity . . . and for the other half too.' It reinforced my views of the unequal power relationship between women and men in both the private and the public domain.

Living in regional Australia I was acutely aware that the sexism was only overshadowed by the racism. I resented the assumptions and arrogance of so many men who at that time controlled both the direction of public policy and its implementation. In many social situations men dominated the debate, whether guffawing loudly around the inevitable beer keg at family barbecues or imposing their predictable opinions in dinner party conversations. It was not easy to challenge the patriarchy or even to present alternative ideas about the relationship between women and men. Clearly there was a vast gulf between the world of feminist discourse and the rugged macho culture of North Queensland. Any mention of women's liberation in mixed company attracted ridicule and highly offensive sexist jokes, while even among women themselves there were suspicions about the new ideas of challenging traditional roles and behaviour.

I knew I was fortunate to be in a personal relationship with a man who actually accepted feminism. Henry may have been a typical Aussie guy at some stage before our marriage, but our lives together in London and Townsville had enabled us to work as equal partners in caring for our children and managing the household. He had always encouraged me to get involved in my various campaigns of local activism and I could rely on him to be there for the children and to give me personal advice and support.

By the beginning of 1972 a number of feminists in Melbourne and Sydney had come together to plan a strategy to get women's issues on the political agenda in the lead-up to the federal election later that year. They formed Women's Electoral Lobby and adopted five key areas for reform – equal pay, equal employment opportunity, contraception services, abortion on demand and twenty-four hour child care. Many women quickly adopted the concept of lobbying for change and branches formed around Australia, including Townsville. Patti Kendall and I worked together as secretary and publicity officer of WEL Townsville. We incorporated our local government lobbying experience and began to focus on federal and state government policies.

That year I decided to upgrade my position to become a permanent teacher. It was unusual for married women to gain permanency with the Queensland Education Department unless they were widowed or divorced. My reason was purely professional as I could not accept that my marital status limited my career options. I requested permanency, completed the relevant forms and waited some time before an elderly inspector came to spend the day in my classroom. He seemed quite happy with my approach to teaching but suggested a confidential chat in the staff room. He was obviously probing my personal life when he queried my reasons for permanency, saying: 'Now tell me, my dear, why do *you* want permanency when your husband has a good job at the university?' He clearly had no idea that a woman might choose to have a career even when her husband was in secure employment. I don't think he really understood my reasoning but anyway I was rewarded with a permanent position. Before I could celebrate this victory, however, I had yet another hurdle to overcome. While my professional credentials were approved, I had to have a thorough medical examination.

By this time I had my suspicion that I was pregnant with our third child, and I knew the Government Medical Officer would certainly reject my application in these circumstances. I sought permission to have the medical completed by my own doctor, Ian Dickson, who had delivered Anna. I told him my dilemma, doubting that he could avoid the inevitable addition to my health status report. He checked all the bureaucratic requirements, confirmed my pregnancy and signed the form saying: 'I am only required to state that you are in good health and I have no doubt about that.' As a result I was probably one of the first married women in Queensland to receive both permanency and 'accouchement' leave in quick succession.

We decided it was time we settled down and bought our own home. We had rented various flats and houses during our first seven years in Townsville, but with a third child due it seemed timely to purchase. We chose an old Queenslander set in a rambling garden at the bottom of Stanton Hill. The price was higher than we could afford, but we borrowed from our parents and had a mortgage approved. We had neglected to consider extras like stamp duty and lawyer's fees so we found ourselves needing a further $1000. I decided to try applying for an overdraft in my own right. I was not confident this would be acceptable, as only a few months earlier I had been obliged to set aside my feminist pride in order to get Henry's signature to open a David Jones account. Battling the patriarchy was all very well, but sometimes it was necessary to confront its reality! Even though I was earning an income, few businesses gave credit to married women without their husband's permission.

I made an appointment with my branch manager, dressed discreetly to try to hide my six months pregnancy and took details of my fortnightly salary. He was very businesslike and agreed without asking any awkward questions. I thought I had succeeded in disguising my condition until I was leaving the interview when he said 'good luck with the new baby'. Clearly, attitudes were changing and I not only gained an overdraft in my own name, but the bank has retained a loyal customer for many years.

Gough Whitlam's 'It's Time' campaign slogan for the 1972 federal election captured the mood for social change across Australia and the Labor Party was elected for the first time in twenty-three years. Whitlam understood the importance of women's support in his electoral success. Few women of my generation will forget the impact of that speech when he addressed the nation with the words 'Men and women of Australia . . .' Today it may seem just a small gesture, but in 1972 it was significant recognition of women and indicated that equality was at last on the political agenda.

As a relatively new member of the Labor party this was my first experience of a victory. In Townsville I was familiar only with being in a minority, so I was excited to feel part of a national majority which promised dynamic change. Those early decisions of the new government were dramatic, particularly the end of conscription and the announcement that Australian troops would return from Vietnam. The appointment of Elizabeth Reid as the Prime Minister's Special Adviser was a signal that many of the issues identified by Women's Electoral Lobby would be included in the new government's plan of social reform.

Rebecca was born in Launceston, Tasmania, at the end of our summer holidays in February 1973. I had arranged to escape the North Queensland heat for the last few weeks of my pregnancy, so our families were able to welcome the new baby before we went home to Townsville. I had no special plans for returning to the classroom as my unpaid leave provision gave me twelve months to decide. There was plenty to do in settling into our new house so I anticipated a year at home. However, when Rebecca was three months old, I was asked to consider joining a James Cook University Education Faculty team overseeing a 'behaviour modification' research project at Central School, near where John and Anna were already enrolled. So I arranged a regular babysitter, Mrs Hurst, to be at home with Rebecca and went back teaching.

The research project required me to teach selected children who were not making progress with their schoolwork and whose behaviour was disruptive in the classroom. Each day this group of children was 'withdrawn' for an hour and a half of specialist teaching which included a system of rewards for good behaviour. I enjoyed the six months project working with 15 five to twelve year olds who attended my specially designed 'resource room' in three age-related groups each day. The research demonstrated the importance of individual teaching and was successful in regard to both the academic progress of the children and their general behaviour when they returned to their regular classrooms.

When Rebecca was six months old she was enrolled at a nearby private childcare centre. At the time several women colleagues were openly critical about my decision, with one saying sweetly: 'Oh dear, I don't know how you can bear to be parted from such a dear little baby.' Had this been said to me in London in 1964 I would have worried and questioned my choice, but this was 1973, when child care was part of feminist advocacy and even the prime minister was listening. There were ongoing debates about the merits of working mothers and many people were critical of young children being placed in day care. Over the years our three children have experienced a variety of childcare services, not all of which would measure up to the more stringent quality standards expected today. Henry and I have never doubted that we made the right decision to rely on child care for our family. I do recognise that our respective jobs gave us greater flexibility to enable us to combine work and family responsibilities, but as a teacher I am convinced that early childhood education provides youngsters with vital learning and socialising experiences.

Throughout 1973 and 1974 a range of women's policies were introduced. For the first time a Federal Government funded sex education and family planning clinics while also lowering the cost of contraceptives. Various types of women's centres were developed to provide advice and support on a range of issues. The supporting mother's benefit was introduced and pensions for single mothers, deserted wives and widows increased. The Children's Commission was established to develop community-based child care and the Family Law Court instituted major divorce law reform. A network of women's refuges and rape crisis centres expanded over this period. In addition women's entitlement to equal pay was accepted and discrimination in employment and working women's needs became the focus of government attention. It was a time of considerable debate and activism to defend some of the new ideas. In North Queensland opposition was formidable as many influential people resisted social change that included talk of sexual equality.

WEL Townsville had been involved in monitoring the social policies of the Whitlam Government and wanted to contrast some of those fresh initiatives with the failures of the Queensland Government. We had experimented with questionnaires and personal interviews with candidates but were disappointed with the poor response and bland rhetoric. Finally we decided something very different was needed to make an impact on the 1974 state election campaign. The result was the Women's Electoral Lobby Cocktail Party and Forum, held at the Hotel Allen in Townsville. We printed gilt-edged invitation cards to announce:

WEL Townsville
cordially invites you to attend a
Cocktail Party
and
Forum
to debate
Women's Issues
prior to the forthcoming
State Election

We invited the three local state parliamentarians as well as several hopeful candidates challenging them for their positions. Many of us wondered if the invitation would really attract the all-male contingent to front up for sherry and olives followed by questioning from an audience of women. It was indeed an unlikely scenario for North Queensland. Yet aspiring politicians understood this was a unique opportunity to promote themselves and their policies, so responded quite enthusiastically. Sitting members were more reluctant, but on the night all candidates were present – no doubt driven by a measure of curiosity.

We had agreed to 'dress up' for the occasion so we discarded our jeans and flowing Indian skirts in favour of the more stylish dresses we had hidden away in our wardrobes. Our members looked eminently respectable in their assorted outfits – so much so we almost failed to recognise each other – but we knew we were making quite an impression on our guests. We conversed politely as the waiters circulated with trays of savouries and drinks. This role reversal was uncommon at the time, but we had insisted that only men be employed for this special evening, as we wanted all women to be free to participate. I don't think any female staff member came to our forum but we were at a very ideological stage of promoting women's rights and saw it as a basic principle that for once men should be in a subservient position.

Then it was down to the serious business of the forum. Local WEL member Dale Spender, looking splendid in diaphanous green, took the chair as the candidates sat uneasily on the raised platform facing a large audience of women aged eight to eighty. Each candidate was invited to outline their party's women's policy for a few minutes before specific questioning began. The speeches from most of the older men were abysmal; they constantly referred to 'you ladies' and obviously had no idea about our concerns. Several talked about their wives and daughters in rambling monotones suggesting they didn't even understand their own families so had no concept of more general women's policy. The younger candidates were better informed and launched into some spirited debate but the older local state parliamentarians were obviously out of their depth.

The questioning was confident and articulate as women from

various backgrounds confronted these men who sought to represent them. Not surprisingly, a number of our guests were intimidated by the sight of 150 women sitting in apparent judgment on their performance. Several were defensive and most displayed a total ignorance of topics relating to women's health and employment prospects, child care and law reform. But the controversial question of the evening came from my friend Janet Greenwood. She was heavily pregnant and looking forward to the birth of her twins, but confused our guests by asking their attitude to the decriminalisation of abortion. Only one of the candidates, John Lamb, a progressive candidate for the Australia Party, dared to honestly declare his support for a woman's right to choose while the remainder made self-righteous speeches in support of the status quo.

I am not sure we changed any attitudes among the candidates that night, but the general level of apathy and arrogance towards women's issues disillusioned Townsville women. We did not make any impact on the outcome of that election, which reinstated the National Party Government. However, our experience made a significant impression on a number of us who resolved to become more actively involved through membership of political parties and nomination for preselection.

In 1975, a few months after the forum, Tom Aikens, Independent Member for Townsville, made a particularly strident speech attacking WEL Townsville under parliamentary privilege. It was International Women's Year and he was aware that the Queensland Government was introducing legislation about women.

> . . . although this is Women's International Year that is not a high sign for the Government to go completely berserk as it is doing and be stampeded at the instigation of little loud-mouthed organisations such as Women's Electoral Lobby.

He was obviously upset that the reform being introduced related to women not needing to state their marital status when applying for employment or any other business transaction. His tirade against WEL continued:

> . . . I am getting sick and tired of this loud-mouthed pressure group that calls itself the Women's Electoral Lobby, which was responsible for stampeding the Minister for Justice into introducing this Bill. We had an experience of them in Townsville during the last election campaign when they wrote to the 12 or 13 candidates for the three Townsville seats and asked us to present ourselves to them so that they could cross-examine us.

His antipathy to women who wanted change was clear in his description of WEL members as he imagined them, contrasting them with 'ordinary women':

> Almost all members of the Women's Electoral Lobby in Townsville are attached to the university in some way or another. We should consider the ordinary women – the workers, the toilers, women in offices and in homes who do the jobs women are supposed to do and are good wives and mothers. They are the women I am concerned about. They do not run along to public meetings.

His vitriolic speech continued as he proceeded to accuse WEL members of drunken behaviour and harassment, but it was his grossly offensive statement about rape which attracted media attention when he asserted: 'Probably some members of the Women's Electoral Lobby would feel rather elated if they themselves were raped!'

I was invited to take part in an ABC televised debate to respond to his outrageous comments. I seriously doubted I had the courage to confront our critic because Tom Aikens was well known for his abrasive style, which he used to threaten and ridicule his opponents. I had no experience of debating and certainly did not relish the thought of confronting Tom on television. Yet I knew that this appalling speech had to be answered. Despite my anxiety at the beginning of the interview, once I got started I began to enjoy myself. The young male interviewer was determined to get some form of apology and Tom Aikens himself was surprisingly unprepared to repeat his accusation on camera. Consequently I emerged from the studio feeling somewhat triumphant. There was no retraction or apology, but I had been able to present rational arguments against this ageing misogynist and hopefully in the process give a good account of Women's Electoral Lobby. The debate gave me a considerable boost in confidence and I began to think more seriously about a political career.

In 1975, for International Women's Year (IWY), I was able to persuade a new editor of the *Townsville Daily Bulletin* to run a series of articles written by women in our own special news column, which highlighted the United Nations logo depicting peace and equality. It was a major breakthrough in my relationship with that newspaper and reflected some progress in the acceptance of Women's Electoral Lobby locally. We were also able to run a special IWY guest speaker series, bringing prominent women like Quentin Bryce and Dorothy MacMahon to Townsville to assist in promoting fresh ideas about the role of women in Australian society.

A group of us led by Townsville Deputy Mayor, Joan Innes Reid, attended the IWY 'Women and Politics' conference in Canberra, where we enthusiastically joined the hundreds of women participating from all over Australia. The conference was an exciting experience, meeting with so many women of all ages and backgrounds within the political environment of the national capital. It was my first visit to Canberra and to Parliament House. The reception in Kings Hall was especially memorable because it was the first time Australian women were in an overwhelming majority at an official reception hosted by the prime minister. Our invitations stated that the dress code was 'lounge suit', so several women borrowed men's suits for the occasion. Throughout the conference we were urged to take action for reform of Australian society to give women equal opportunity to participate in all areas of working and community life. We were also reminded that Australian women's struggle was part of the global campaign for women's rights. Generally the media reporting of the conference was unfavourable, inaccurate and highly critical of several guest speakers. A large group of women marched in protest to the *Canberra Times* newspaper, where we occupied the office and demanded to see the editor about more accurate reporting. It was an important and historic conference, which deserved more objective media coverage. Like many women who had the opportunity to attend the 'Women and Politics' conference I found my few days there tremendously stimulating. It reinforced my personal commitment to feminism and my determination to work for change in North Queensland.

CHAPTER 7

Getting serious about party politics 1975–1982

THE POTENTIAL FOR social reform which had seemed possible throughout most of International Women's Year came to an abrupt halt when, on 11 November 1975, the Governor-General, John Kerr, sacked Prime Minister Gough Whitlam.

I was at a lunchtime meeting in my special education unit at Central State School where a group of teachers and parents were interviewing applicants for the position of After-school Care Coordinator. We had successfully applied for funds from the new Children's Commission and were preparing to open Townsville's first funded after-school care centre.

We were interrupted by a knock on the door and a colleague announced, 'Guess what, I think the Prime Minister has been sacked'. We rushed to the staffroom, where a number of teachers were listening to a radio update from Canberra. When the details of the dismissal became clear I went to the classrooms of several close colleagues to tell them the news. My final call was to John's class where his teacher, Warren Knight, received the news with such gravity that John thought his baby sister, Rebecca, had been involved in an accident. That night as we watched the historic event described on television John was able to give a running commentary based on his teacher's comprehensive lecture to the class of eleven year olds that afternoon.

The following period was a very volatile one in Australian politics and our family personally experienced some of the rancour and division in the Townsville community. Both Henry and I were well-known Labor supporters as we had the local candidate's election signs in our front garden and car stickers clearly identifying our political loyalty. During that emotional election campaign which followed Whitlam's dismissal we had rocks thrown on our roof and late-night abusive phone calls. Henry was often asked to comment on political issues because he was lecturing in Australian politics. He had hosted university meetings for Gough Whitlam and other visiting ministers, so was clearly seen as aligned to the Labor Government. I was involved in organising at the local ALP branch level. I had also been photographed for newspaper advertisements urging a vote for John Rockett, the Federal Candidate for Herbert. There were only a few people in Townsville at this time to publicly identify with the Labor Party, so it was not really surprising that we attracted opposition.

In the last week of the election campaign supporters of Gough Whitlam gathered at a candlelight vigil for democracy in the Strand Park. It was well attended by mainly family groups enjoying picnic teas at sunset. However later in the evening the children and I watched the wife of a prominent Liberal Party member physically confront a young Labor supporter. He had long hair which she grabbed as she tried to get him to respond. But he wisely put his hands behind his back, refusing to resist in any way. Nevertheless, his attacker later called the police claiming assault. I took the children home, anxious to avoid what had the potential to become a very nasty brawl. Henry was in Sydney so I approached our dark, empty house with a degree of nervousness.

I settled the children and went to bed but was disturbed by abusive voices and car headlights shining in to our bedroom window. John was not asleep so together we watched several cars screeching up and down outside our home. I rang the police but their response was that they were short-staffed and would send a car as soon as possible. I realised I would not sleep if we remained at home so I woke the girls, bundled the three children into the car and headed to my friend's home for the night. A car followed us to the nearby street where Janet and I opened a bottle of wine and watched over our combined brood of eight until the early hours of the morning. Other known Whitlam supporters were similarly targeted in that period between the dismissal and the election.

Prior to the 1975 election an ad hoc national grouping of women supporting Gough Whitlam was formed in response to the genuine efforts of his government to initiate women's policy reform and the support given to women's organisations during International Women's Year. Someone I had met at the 'Women and Politics' conference in Canberra phoned me and asked me to be the local contact for the Women for Whitlam campaign. I was sent details of radio and newspaper advertising that featured slogans about Labor's health and education policies. I arranged for these to be included in our local campaign in support of candidate John Rockett. It was also suggested that we could publicly identify this campaign by handing out red poppies to remind voters that the dismissal had taken place on Remembrance Day. I was sent a large box of poppies to be worn up until the election. However, not surprisingly, the reaction of many locals to this symbolism was extremely negative, so after several irate exchanges I packed up the poppies and delivered them to the Townsville Returned Services League with a message that they were a donation from the Australian Labor Party. Perhaps the greatest lesson I learnt in those years was strategic political compromise.

I remember that night of the 1975 election as a very depressing occasion. The children and I had flown from Townsville at the beginning of the school holidays to join Henry in Sydney, where we were staying en route to a family Christmas in Tasmania. We watched the disastrous events unfold on the television in our hotel room. I was exhausted from a particularly frantic year of teaching and organising International Women's Year events. The final month of campaigning had been especially demanding, so my disappointment and frustration were particularly intense. To me it seemed that so many reforms would be halted by a change of government. All our efforts in areas of social policy advocacy appeared fruitless and the circumstances of the Whitlam dismissal undermined my faith in the political process.

My increased political activism during International Women's Year led me to nominate as a Labor candidate for the state seat of Townsville early in 1976. I was persuaded to contest preselection by friends Kett Kennedy and John Rockett, though I suspect they may have been mischievously urging me on in order to upset the favourite contender, Geoff Smith. Both Kett and John were very familiar with political scheming in the Queensland Labor Party but they also saw an opportunity for a new style of candidate. When it was first suggested I should 'throw my hat in the ring' I was very doubtful. By this time I was determined to run for local council but State Parliament seemed too ambitious. My two male mentors reminded me of my vocal advocacy for women's active participation at all levels of society. They quoted the International Women's Year slogan: 'A Woman's Place is in the House and in the Senate too' and told me to practise what I preached.

Still I was unsure. The children were quite young – eleven,

nine and three – and that year we had planned to be in London for Henry's six-month sabbatical leave from James Cook University. I had made my own arrangements for leave to study special education in Sweden and the United Kingdom. Yet I knew that opportunities in politics were rare and that I had to at least indicate my longer-term intentions. I finally rationalised my decision to nominate, knowing I was very unlikely to defeat the preferred male candidate at the preselection stage. Nevertheless, I knew it would be a good opportunity to gain knowledge of the process and indicate to local party members I was serious about future preselections.

I left my nomination until the last minute and had to hand-deliver it early on the due date. That morning was a particularly chaotic one in our household. There was a major dispute between John and Anna, Rebecca had lost her sandals and Henry was reminding me he needed the car that day. Four people were demanding my attention when I announced that I had to go out before breakfast. I sat in the car for a few minutes listening to the general pandemonium I was leaving behind. Slowly I put the key into the ignition and wondered how I could possibly make a serious bid for preselection at that stage of my life, when the immediate demands of my family were so obvious. I hesitated and almost changed my mind but then turned the key and revved the engine, drowning out the sounds of domestic disruption, and drove off to submit my nomination.

My decision made little impact at home, but sent shockwaves through the Australian Labor Party locally and ultimately involved the Queensland party hierarchy in heated arguments about my eligibility as a potential candidate. In 1976 only a few women had ever nominated for Labor preselection in Queensland and only one – Vi Jordan, Member for Ipswich – had been elected. She described the reaction to her admission to the all-male domain with the comment: 'They regard me as a porcupine'.

My nomination certainly seemed to needle a number of Labor Party members. My actual opponent, Geoff Smith, was apparently relaxed about the competition but a number of his supporters were furious especially that 'an uppity sheila' should challenge him. While I had been active in several election campaigns I was not a typical member. The convoluted processes of the very macho culture were tedious and I was more interested in getting involved in local issues affecting women and Aborigines. I resisted the accepted female role of tea-making and had no idea how many loaves of bread were needed to make sandwiches for sixty. I was out of step with the expectations of many members because my focus was on those areas of political activism in which I could achieve some change. A number of members thought me 'too academic'. Furthermore, my lack of fundraising skills attracted considerable criticism. While I had been an enthusiastic fundraiser for my work with disabled and Aboriginal children, I had become much more interested in policy and resented being asked to confine my political contribution to fundraising.

I soon realised there would be a determined effort to prevent my nomination proceeding. What started as a whispering campaign against me developed into a furore of activity to discredit my credentials as a potential candidate. There was a dispute about the continuity of my membership and some of my critics accused me of disloyalty during the local government elections held earlier that year. Deputy Mayor Joan Innes Reid had nominated as an independent mayoral candidate. Like me she had been inspired by International Women's Year and thought it was time a woman ran for the top job in council. However this put her up against the leader of the Labor Party council team, Perc Tucker. I had faced this conflict of loyalties by talking directly to her and explaining that as an ALP member I had to support the Labor team. She understood my dilemma and we both knew there was a similarity in our respective policies. Many women were actively working for Joan and because I was part of the local women's movement some party members assumed I must be part of her support group. Labor won both the mayoralty and the majority on the council that year, so in fact some of my feminist friends were critical that it was the Labor Party which prevented Joan continuing her good work on council. It would not be the last time my feminism conflicted with party loyalty.

As branch members debated whether or not my nomination should be accepted I discovered that the demands of my family on that fateful morning of my nomination were insignificant when compared with the strident opposition from some of my ALP critics. My own supporters were indignant about the strenuous efforts of the opponents who were determined to prevent a contest between old- and new-style candidates. After considerable uproar locally I was obliged to make a personal statement, which was forwarded to the Brisbane-based ALP office:

> It concerns me that there has been a concerted effort among many members of the ALP in Townsville to obstruct my nomination for Townsville West. Allegations without foundation have been levelled against me and have been publicly refuted at branch meetings. My commitment is to the Labor Party and I see that the petty jealousy between individuals has no place in the vital business of winning elections. I would ask that, in accordance with the democratic principles of the Labor movement, I be allowed to exercise my right as a member to put myself forward in a plebiscite, so that the members can decide whom they see as the best candidate to represent Labor policy.

I thought this would help bring the issue to some formal conclusion. I wanted to either get on with preparing for the party members' vote or be told formally my candidature was unacceptable. We had made our overseas travel bookings, so time was running out and I felt the delay was deliberate to force me to withdraw. Finally my nomination was accepted and the ballot was held when we were in London. Despite the rigorous efforts of my supporters I lost to Geoff Smith who went on to become a minister in the Goss Government.

Looking back after more than thirty years membership of the Labor Party, I can only marvel at my determination to continue with that first nomination. In retrospect it was probably foolish to imagine that I could seriously manage my plans for that year with an initial preselection bid. It was such a challenge to the status quo for a woman to dare nominate against the popular man expected to take the position. I had an activist feminist background *and* I was planning to travel overseas. Yet it is possible that, had I not experienced that particular preselection battle in 1976, I may not have been sufficiently motivated to try again. Politics is inevitably about timing and the impression one makes in particular circumstances. I had moved outside my comfort zone by daring to seek consideration as a candidate for State Parliament so I knew there would be a 'next time' and it had to be a little less difficult the second time around.

That year our family spent six months in London for Henry's sabbatical leave. We rented a small two-bedroom flat in Islington and the three children went to school – John to Archway Secondary School and the girls to the local primary school and kindergarten. I spent two weeks in Stockholm as guest of the Swedish Institute where I learnt about trends in the integration of children with disabilities into regular schools. It was my first trip away alone and, although I was excited, it was daunting to arrive in Stockholm on a dark evening in October and have to find my way to a hotel on the edge of the city. I was shown a tiny, neat room and advised that breakfast would be served on the first floor. It was only about 6 pm and I was hungry but my hotel did not offer an evening meal. My friendly host gave me a street map and marked several restaurants. I returned to my room, feeling unsure about venturing out into a strange city. Finally I decided I had to make the effort to explore that night so I headed out into the capital.

Stockholm was a very pleasant safe city for a woman travelling on her own, or that was certainly my experience in 1976. I walked for miles throughout the city, day and night, and had none of the hassles I may have expected back in Australia or London. My Swedish Institute hosts invited me to their homes and taught me to skate on the big outdoor rink in the heart of the city. I was most impressed with the educational part of my visit because schools were so well equipped and staffed to meet the needs of children with varying disabilities. Integration policy was achieving great results in Sweden at that time because there were adequate financial resources allocated to ensure the policy succeeded.

When we returned to Townsville in 1977 I completed my Diploma in Special Education at James Cook University and began tutoring at the Townsville College of Advanced Education. My appointment coincided with the first intake of mature-age Aboriginal and Torres Strait Islander students who had worked as teacher assistants on Cape York and throughout the Torres Strait. I was responsible for first- and second-year classes in Language and Literature, which required me to give students practical experience in the teaching of reading and literacy skills. During this period I was able to undertake some research at the Black Community School, a primary school that had been established in 1973 by Eddie Mabo and Burnum Burnum, an Aboriginal activist from New South Wales. It followed the success of Kindergarten Headstart. Parents wanted their children to continue learning within their own culture because they were dissatisfied with the way they were treated in the Queensland Education system.

When the Black Community School opened the *Townsville Daily Bulletin* headline on the front page was: 'Motives of City's Black School Justifiably Suspicious'. The article went on to quote the Queensland Minister for Education, who was openly hostile to the idea that Indigenous parents were opting out of the state system to try to provide a more culturally supportive learning environment. He warned parents: 'people attempting to entice children away from a State primary school . . . were technically guilty of an offence and risked prosecution'.

In changing community attitudes to this new venture I thought it was important to have some evidence-based research to endorse the apparent success of the new school. I was interested to test the basic skills of children on entry from state primary schools and compare the results after a year in their new environment, so I visited the school at the beginning and end of the year testing children's language, numeracy and comprehension skills. I found there was in fact a significant improvement in their results. In addition, the overall social benefits of the school and particularly the participation of parents in cultural maintenance demonstrated the importance of this innovative educational venture. It in fact experimented with many of the ideas to be adopted in Australian Aboriginal education policy over the next twenty years.

After returning from London in 1977 I decided to be much more patient in complying with Labor Party processes and expectations. At one branch meeting the all-male membership was debating the major fundraising effort – a hotel raffle held every Saturday morning. The problem seemed to be insufficient numbers of volunteers to sell the tickets in the 'meat tray', which consisted of several large steaks donated by the local Australian Meat Workers Union. The branch secretary called for members to nominate for the roster, so I indicated I was available. The list of names was read back – Fred, Bill, Dave . . . I interrupted to report my name was missing but was told: 'You can't go into the bar to sell raffle tickets'. The time had come to challenge this double standard. I made a short but pointed speech reminding members that in the 1976 preselection I had been criticised for failing to be involved in fundraising. There was silence until a young man finally said: 'Fair enough, why not give her a go?' For the next two years I spent most Saturday mornings in the bar of the Centenary Hotel in the suburb of Currajong and was quite successful selling those raffle tickets. This apprenticeship seemed to prove that I did have the appropriate credentials to be considered as a candidate this time at local government level

My second attempt at preselection followed in 1978, when I gained a place on the Townsville City Council team – Tucker's Ten – which was elected in its entirety in March 1979. After I was elected to the council I found our family life suddenly became public. Not only did the phone ring constantly, but we had unannounced callers at all hours of the day and night. Everywhere we went as a family someone wanted to talk to me about their particular grievance. Whether it was potholes or uncollected rubbish, speeding trucks or overhanging branches, I was expected to be both knowledgeable and responsive. Complaints and enquiries interrupted meals or rare times of relaxation. When we went to town, ratepayers stopped to talk at length about their particular concern or offer advice. I was unfazed by all these extra demands and enjoyed the challenge of trying to resolve the most intransigent problems.

If my family objected at times they were usually accepting about the intrusion into their lives and each in their own way adapted to the new demands placed on them. Many families find these kinds of pressure unacceptable and such conflict between personal and public roles can lead to serious alienation. Both partners and children can resent competing for time with the family member who is a public figure. Furthermore the scrutiny of media and ever-present critics can put pressure on personal relationships. It is still a major disincentive for many women contemplating public life.

When I was elected to council, Henry and I were each very involved in our work and various other commitments. I was completing an external studies course in government and public policy at the University of Queensland while Henry was finishing his first book, *The Other Side of the Frontier.* The children had the usual round of after-school and weekend activities so it needed a great deal of organisation to balance competing needs. We lived close to the city centre and council chambers so I was able to get home between some meetings. Henry had taken over shopping and cooking a few years earlier, when I went back to university and had late classes. We employed a cleaner and the children were expected to check the roster on the fridge to do their share of chores. I persuaded John that as a secondary school pupil, he should now be ironing his own shirts and many years later he is far more competent at the ironing board than me. Anna was expected to make her own and Rebecca's school lunch every day. One friend was surprised that we expected our children to contribute in this way, but it seemed a sensible way to run a busy household. At an early age, even Rebecca wanted to be included, though obviously the novelty wore off as she got older. Of course the Reynolds family did *not* run like clockwork and we endured the usual arguments and disputes common to any family, but we did endeavour to make a commitment to equal sharing of responsibility.

We also tried to avoid narrow sex-role stereotyping within the family, but community expectations could not always be avoided. When I was first elected the local media came in search of typical images of the 'housewife' who had joined the council and insisted I pose for a photo in MY kitchen. The television crew also rejected filming me at work in my home office because it would appear 'too dull', so instead I had to pretend I had all the time in the world to stroll in our tropical garden.

As a member of the Townsville City Council I learned quickly about the relationship between council bureaucracy and elected representatives. In describing one of my first meetings to my mother I wrote: 'I attended my first Health Committee meeting and was appalled at the size of the agenda but more particularly the rate at which the bureaucrats have us race through it! All decisions are virtually made by Council officers but have to be ratified by our committee.'

One of my first campaigns was to try to introduce recycling. I was appalled to discover that anyone scavenging for useful items on the city dump would be prosecuted. This seemed unnecessarily harsh and also wasteful, as many people discarded goods that could be used by others. Over the next few years I advocated reform and eventually a recycling policy was adopted. It was not the kind of victory that some of my feminist friends thought worth pursuing – should one really waste time and energy challenging male dominance over loads of local rubbish? My personal commitment as a feminist had not changed and I was still lobbying for the recognition of women. However the reality of local government required active participation in the day-to-day management of a community and I was learning to set aside some of my more strident rhetoric in favour of more subtle and persuasive argument. I still wanted to change the world (or at least my small part of it) but I was starting to appreciate that this had to be a very long-term goal.

In those early months on the Townsville City Council I was preoccupied with health and safety issues. I advocated an enhanced vaccination program against rubella, developed a bike safety campaign and attended a National Childhood Accident Prevention conference. It was International Year of the Child so I was able to encourage council to become more proactive around issues affecting children. I chaired a special committee responsible for overseeing the development of the city's bikeways and organised a major education safety campaign for cyclists and motorists. I made speeches about the fencing of swimming pools and compulsory child restraints in cars.

During these years the Townsville City Council was probably the most socially progressive in Queensland. It included three women, Sheila Keeffe, Delma Benson and me, each of whom was vocal in championing social justice – a term unknown in Queensland politics at the time. Mike Reynolds, a social worker, became mayor and we appointed a social planner to expand a number of community development programs that catered for homeless women and children and unemployed youth. The council made ongoing representations to State and Federal Governments to support Aborigines and Torres Strait Islanders, the most vulnerable of Townsville's citizens. I promoted the idea of an Aboriginal and Islander Liaison Officer and one was appointed in 1982 to help overcome the lack of state and federal government services in the city. We upgraded facilities for the Aboriginal fringe community of Happy Valley and worked towards local management of the Aitkenvale Aboriginal Hostel. Indigenous culture was incorporated into city events and exhibitions. Despite our efforts a number of policies failed to attract financial support because of the apparent disinterest of decision makers based in Brisbane and Canberra. It was not unusual for the Townsville City Council to be querying the policies of State and Federal Governments in the early 1980s. Development and environment issues, together with social policy, were prominent in conflicts between the Townsville City Council and the Bjelke-Petersen National Party Government. I learned a great deal about inter-government relations and the extent to which local government could be overridden.

The location of a seventy-three metre chimney at the Townsville Hospital created one such conflict. There was a storm of protest from residents, angry at both the polluting and the aesthetic impacts of such a dominating addition to the city skyline. Medical authorities and the Air Pollution Control Council warned of public health risks but the National Party–appointed hospital board was adamant that the project should proceed. We lived just behind the hospital, so I joined with the newly formed residents group to try various ways of changing this decision.

The controversy raged for several months and National Party delegates to the state conference in Townsville were confronted by a half-page newspaper advertisement we organised, featuring an artist's impression of the offending tower. Despite many meetings and letters of protest we were unsuccessful and the monstrous structure was finally erected and began continuously belching black smoke across our suburb.

In 1981 Townsville probably became the first Australian city to officially fly the Aboriginal flag alongside the national flag in the centre of the city mall. That flag was a gift from the North Queensland Land Council in appreciation of the council's support in developing policy that recognised Aborigines and Torres Strait Islanders. Shorty O'Neil, an executive member of the land council, presented the flag to me and we raised it together in a small ceremony watched by just a handful of local people. However, the reaction over the next few weeks was distressingly vindictive as people phoned and wrote to express their disgust at my acceptance of the flag. In State Parliament, Aboriginal and Islander Affairs Minister Tomkins strongly criticised me and said the Aboriginal flag was a symbol of division in Australian society. I continued to defend the council's flying of the flag, pointing out that: 'Aborigines have as much right to a flag to highlight their identity as any other ethnic group, sporting club or business'. It took nearly another twenty years for the flying of the Aboriginal flag to be accepted around Australia so I am proud to have been part of that initial flag-raising.

My four years in local government in Townsville were invaluable in teaching me how to work politically within a bureaucracy. I learnt much more about party politics and my eyes were opened to the way bureaucrats try to maintain control regardless of elected representatives' priorities.

My work led to my becoming responsible for community and cultural development in the city and that involved liaising with state and federal government departments, the Australian Broadcasting Commission and the Australia Council. Our council built the Townsville Civic Theatre and bought a grand old bank building which was restored as a regional art gallery. Together with other councils in the region we established 'New Moon', the North Queensland Theatre Company, and encouraged the establishment of 'Dance North', a local modern dance company. Townsville City Council employed a Community Arts Officer and ran vacation care programs several years before such activities were expected of Queensland local government.

Yet, despite these major endeavours, Townsville was regarded 'down south' as an insignificant small town. A number of state and federal public servants were openly dismissive of our efforts.

At this time many of them failed to recognise the importance of regional policy initiatives and did not appreciate that people in regional Queensland did not have access to comparable standards of services and the facilities that were taken for granted in Brisbane. It was an important period for me in discovering how to manoeuvre around barriers when confronted by bureaucrats who resisted change in the delivery of public policy, especially to regional population centres.

CHAPTER 8

Parliamentary politics 1983

1983 WAS TO have been the year I spent more time at home with my family. I had plans to do some part-time lecturing and continue with my council work but I had made promises to them about baking bread and catching up on neglected jobs around the house.

My good intentions were overtaken by a remarkable series of events in Canberra late in January of that year. Bob Hawke challenged Bill Hayden for leadership of the Labor Party, and Prime Minister Malcolm Fraser announced a double dissolution election. North Queensland Senator Jim Keeffe decided to resign as he did not want to serve another six-year term and, within two days of his announcement, my name appeared in southern newspapers as a 'certainty' to fill the vacancy. Jim had phoned to tell me he was about to announce his resignation and urged me to get a nomination in that day. Soon after I had similar calls from Denis Murphy, State President, and Peter Beattie, State Secretary of the Labor Party, who both told me that the ALP National Executive would have to make the decision about the Queensland vacancy because the campaign was already under way, so there was no time for standard rank and file preselection.

In my case, that was a tremendous advantage, as the Brisbane-dominated factional system of the day would not have endorsed a female outsider from the North. In fact, my elevation by the National Executive created a great deal of hostility towards me, and this lingered, creating problems in my next preselection. Several members of the National Executive knew me because of my work as North Queensland Party Organiser and Campaign Director for the Labor candidate in the Herbert electorate, Ted Lindsay. Apparently a number of them spoke on my behalf at the special meeting of the National Executive. They reminded members that it was important to replace Jim Keeffe with a northerner – and a woman candidate in that particular election was seen as a bonus.

My sudden elevation to a guaranteed position on the Labor Senate ticket amazed me and gave me little time to dwell on the implications of the momentous change in my life. Henry was away when he read the first report of my likely success and by the end of the week, when he returned, I was already the endorsed candidate. The children dutifully posed for photos and seemed really excited about all the attention.

Locally, the decision was popular and I received many phone calls, flowers and cards of congratulations – even before I was elected. Many people were genuinely pleased that the ALP had made a preselection decision that discriminated in favour of a woman from a regional area. It was both a help and a hindrance in my future career, with my critics claiming I was a token woman or only promoted because I came from North Queensland.

The *Townsville Daily Bulletin* published a glowing editorial welcoming the decision. It enthused: 'Alderman Reynolds' selection for a winnable position on the ticket also maintains the ALP's oft-stated commitment to recognition of the importance of women in politics as well as in other fields'.

Given my relationship with the *Townsville Daily Bulletin*, this level of support reflected a new political climate developing in the northern city. The suspicions of left-wing conspiracies emanating from the Whitlam years had long since faded. Now the fresh ideas of Labor's Shadow Ministry, consistently promoted over the period 1980–1983, seemed realistic and acceptable. The steady progress made over six years by an ALP Townsville City Council had created a ready acceptance of Labor's capacity to govern locally and this, in turn, enhanced perceptions about a new Labor administration in Canberra.

My life changed dramatically as I responded to the demand of campaign priorities. I flew to Brisbane for the launching of the Queensland senate team and spent much of the day being interviewed. The campaign was frenetic because I was scheduled to travel all over Queensland and interstate, meeting people, making speeches and trying to catch up on my knowledge of Labor policy. There was a feeling of expectation and excitement on the campaign trail. Bob Hawke was a popular figure and I sensed an element of Whitlam's 'It's Time' slogan as I talked to people who seemed confident of a Labor victory.

In Townsville, we planned a major political rally for the new leader's campaign launch in North Queensland. It was held in the forecourt of the City Council building, where we organised seating for about two hundred people and hired a bush band to entertain people. The crowd that gathered that steamy tropical night in February was quite phenomenal: families, workers, students and business leaders. Men, women and children – all streamed into the open space in such numbers that any casual observer would have assumed they were attending a football match or a pop concert. They filled the designated area and, after the estimated numbers reached well over a thousand, they took over the intersection outside, forcing police to close two roads and divert traffic.

My job as MC for the night was to introduce local speakers and encourage the audience to sing along with the bush band. After an hour, I was running out of ideas to keep the huge crowd entertained. I was hot and sweaty from urging the crowd to sing *Click Go the Shears* yet again and still there was no sign of our special guest. A rainstorm had delayed the flight from Cairns, so Hawke's party was well behind schedule. The band needed a break, so there I was alone with a microphone and a restless crowd. I launched into an ad hoc outline of the Labor Party's pre-election commitments and tried to give a reasonable performance but it was getting late and I wasn't the star attraction. At last I saw a fleet of cars arriving, so with some considerable relief I gave the rallying call we had all been waiting for: 'Ladies and gentlemen, please welcome the next Prime Minister of Australia, Bob Hawke'.

People went wild with enthusiasm as they clapped and cheered. A deafening chant began as the slogan 'Give Bob the Job' was shouted as a welcome. I stood in front of that expectant crowd wondering if the man they wanted would ever appear. Many people surged forward to shake hands and Hawke, surrounded by fans, took what seemed like an eternity to finally reach the stage. His presence and rousing speech of commitment to North Queensland were greeted with more rapturous applause and we finished up the night with the crowd still roaring their approval.

At my first Brisbane press conference as number four on the Queensland senate team, I talked about trying to present an alternative image of the North. The ultra-conservative and reactionary policies of the Bjelke-Petersen years had created Australia's own 'deep North', renowned for the extremism of a premier who relied on the notorious electoral gerrymander to dominate politics. In outlining my personal goals, I emphasised the importance of women in political life, my commitment to Aborigines and Torres Strait Islanders and people living in regional Queensland. Clearly, these issues did not rate with the media and most questioning was aimed at prolonging the 'shock' impact of the ALP's decision to appoint this untested Townsville woman to a safe position in the Senate. Some interrogation was openly hostile, while other journalists simply ignored my presence, as if it was of no relevance whatsoever. Obviously, in Brisbane, I did not enjoy the effusive support of my local media.

The 1983 federal election campaign was especially focused on a reform agenda in health, employment, social welfare and education. The withdrawal of federal funds from Queensland's hospital and health services had forced higher state charges and waiting periods of up to two years for elective surgery. The free Queensland hospital system was in jeopardy and, at the time, some 37 per cent of the population were not covered by health insurance. The proposed Medicare system, through which universal health cover would be funded by a 1 per cent levy on taxable income, was attractive to many people and yet there remained some scepticism that it would provide any significant improvement in the hospital system. Queenslanders had a reluctance to move away from reliance on their free hospitals and it was not easy to promote the new health proposal.

It was less problematic to advocate social welfare reforms because Queenslanders depended much more on the non-government sector in this area. Coming from a local government that did incorporate social welfare initiatives, I was enthusiastic about the needs-based model planned for state and local government. This policy relied on social justice principles directed at the poor, the elderly and the unemployed, with provisions for increased benefits, including an increase over three years for the old-age pension, to 25 per cent of average weekly earnings.

Regional unemployment also provided a strong campaign focus throughout Queensland. In March 1981, the Federal Government had withdrawn the provision of regional Commonwealth Employment Services on the pretext of cost cutting. While Queensland's unemployment rate of 11 per cent stood above the national average, it did not accurately reflect the job crisis in regional cities. Shadow Minister for Social Security, Don Grimes, sent me data on pension payments, from which I estimated that Cairns had an unemployment rate of 15 per cent and Townsville 12 per cent. In a statement during that election campaign, I expressed concern about 'the growing inequalities of the long-term unemployed living in the shadow of luxurious holiday accommodation'.

It was also my responsibility to promote the North Queensland Policy, which the local campaign committee had been developing with Labor shadow ministers over the period 1980–1983. With its own attractive poster and slogan, 'North Queensland – A Special Place', it reflected the first attempt by a political party to define regional policy in a specific area. The policy identified the fact that 500,000 North Queenslanders lived in an area of strategic significance, which had been overlooked by both State and Federal Governments.

The history of North Queensland reflects strong identification with an area from north of Mackay to the Torres Strait, and there have been various efforts over the years to promote the concept of a separate state. People living in this vast regional area of Queensland had watched successive governments bypass their demands for recognition. Shadow Minister John Button had discussed the strength of this regional feeling with Herbert candidate, Eamon (Ted) Lindsay, Henry and me, so we were able to convince him to develop a policy which responded to local expectations. The key commitments of the North Queensland Policy included tourism, transport and infrastructure and indicated initiatives designed to respond to the region's needs. We included two major initiatives designed to maximise interest in Labor planning for the region: the construction of the Burdekin Dam, a vital initiative for primary producers in the region, and a commitment to re-establish the Institute of Tropical Medicine at James Cook University.

It was not easy for me to articulate some of this agenda, most of which was unfamiliar territory for me. I began a crash course in trying to comprehend the detail of sales tax, diesel fuel excise, industry loans and the inner workings of the Department of Transport. While inspecting 'black spots' on the Bruce Highway, I listened intently to engineers' assessments of road reconstruction costs that could prevent horrific road accidents on single-lane bridges. I met with cane farmers suffering from the downturn in the international market, trying to remember pricing patterns over previous years so I could make an informed comment about domestic formulas. Despite some obvious scepticism about a woman's capacity to represent their needs, it was pleasantly surprising that my entry into these male-dominated areas received mostly benign tolerance and acceptance. At one particularly volatile meeting in Proserpine, the well-known National Party chairman, usually vocally opposed to the Labor Party, intervened on my behalf saying: 'Give her a go – she's not an expert, you know'.

There were few chances on that 1983 campaign trail to make speeches about the rights of women or Aborigines and little interest in my concerns for the environment. Yet I did manage a couple of media interviews in which I outlined my longstanding commitment to feminism, and emphasised that under the Liberal

Government the gains that women had made during the 1970s were being seriously eroded. Since 1975, when she was elected to the Senate for the ACT, Susan Ryan had been developing a comprehensive Labor Women's Policy that built on the reforms made by the Whitlam Government and brought the Labor Party up to date in its appeal to women voters. All women candidates in the 1983 election were invited to the major Women's Policy launch in Melbourne in the last weeks leading up to that election. Bob Hawke launched the policy with considerable conviction and Susan detailed some of the initiatives in regard to anti-discrimination legislation and a new Status of Women Policy Unit to oversee a range of women's programs. This was a significant shift in image for the ALP, which had been seen as a male-dominated party of the trade union movement with little focus on women.

In the campaign I also focused on environment policies, highlighting my anti-uranium stance and condemning the Federal Government's support for the proposed uranium processing plant on a tributary of the Burdekin River at Ben Lomond, west of Townsville. I also called for the French mining company, Minatome, to cease all mining activity in the catchment of North Australia's most important river system. At the same time the premier was in negotiations to give permits for oil drilling in the vicinity of the Great Barrier Reef, so a number of environment groups were seeking commitment from Queensland candidates that a Labor Government would protect the reef.

On Election Day, 5 March 1983, Anna and Rebecca accompanied me to every polling booth within the Townsville area. This drive took almost the whole day, allowing time to thank patient campaign workers standing in the hot sun handing out 'how to vote' cards. We delivered cool drinks and sandwiches and reminded people to come to the post-election party that night. In addition there were queries and protests about electoral issues as some people's names were not on the roll or they found it difficult to vote outside their electorate. I played the responsible candidate role while the girls in their 'Give Bob the Job' T-shirts shouted slogans and cheered whenever we drove past ALP signs. Henry spent much of the day ferrying older party members to vote and taking various phone calls at home.

The excitement of that day reached fever pitch by evening, when all our workers converged on the campaign headquarters – a high-set old Queenslander due for demolition. We crowded around the television set to watch the preliminary results and, when the swing to Labor was clear, the house itself seemed to sway precariously with the weight of so many cheering supporters. By the time Bob Hawke's victory speech was due we were advising people to celebrate out in the garden, because a local builder had a genuine fear that at the height of celebrations the house might collapse. And then, as if the new prime minister had himself decreed it, the tropical rain broke the local drought and the perpetual drumming on the old tin roof drowned the enthusiastic cheers. We partied well into the next morning, as Labor had not only won government but Eamon Lindsay was the new Member for Herbert and, in Cairns, John Gaylor had become Member for Leichhardt. Our campaign to win two North Queensland seats had been successful and, almost incidentally, Queensland had elected its first Labor woman senator.

During the election campaign it had not escaped my attention that, of the forty-two Queensland senate candidates, just eight were women, but when the final results came in three women had been elected. Liberal Senator Kathy Martin and National Party Senator Flo Bjelke-Petersen were re-elected in 1983 and I commenced my first term in the Australian Senate.

At the official Declaration of the Queensland senate polls held in Brisbane on 29 March, I said that I was honoured to be elected as the first Labor woman senator for Queensland, but the focus of my speech was devoted to policies of the newly elected Federal Government, with a few pointed remarks about the Queensland Premier's comments about Bob Hawke's success.

While overseas, Joh Bjelke-Peterson had made a speech in which he was strongly critical of the Federal Labor Government, and even threatened to secede from the rest of Australia. His hostility to the election of a 'socialist' national government was extreme and he had said his government would adopt a policy of non-cooperation with the Hawke administration. I had prepared my speech to challenge these quite bizarre statements and was heading towards the official event when I met, for the first time, Flo Bjelke-Petersen. She greeted me like an old friend and suddenly I became confused and uncertain about the speech I had so carefully prepared. It had not occurred to me that I might feel uncomfortable being critical of Joh while seated alongside his wife, Lady Flo. But there I was, speech in hand, in the full glare of television lights – and a press release already distributed. I took a deep breath, nodded in the direction of my new colleague and kept to the prepared text.

I always appreciated Flo's special ability to separate her personal support for her controversial husband from her professional relationship with her colleagues. We enjoyed a very harmonious friendship during our years in the Senate and yet, on occasions, it must have been difficult for her to accept some of the more vocal criticism of the Bjelke-Petersen State Government.

My introduction to life in the Australian Parliament involved some juggling of family priorities, which had been overtaken by the election campaign. I had scarcely thought how I was going to manage a complex life of travel to and from Canberra. My mother planned to move from Tasmania to live with us. John had left home to go to university and Anna was in her final year of secondary school. Henry had his own professional life at James Cook University, so Rebecca's routine as a ten-year-old was the one most likely to be affected by my new career. Henry and I decided it was important that she have the opportunity to understand my new role by initially spending time with me in Canberra. I rented a flat in Red Hill and enrolled Rebecca at the primary school opposite.

She spent her late afternoons and evenings in Parliament House, bounding up the front steps after school past demonstrators to show her identity pass to parliamentary attendants. She wandered the corridors or settled herself in my office until dinner in the parliamentary dining room. On late nights, she spent the evening curled up asleep on a makeshift bed in my office. I would wake her, often at midnight, to go home after the Senate had concluded. Rebecca frequently visited Flo's Parliament House office for afternoon tea treats. Growing up in a political household, Rebecca was puzzled that this friendly grandmother could possibly share family connections with the extremely vocal Queensland Premier, so often criticised by her parents. She clearly wanted to rationalise her understanding of politics and concluded: 'Well, Senator Bjelke-Petersen is my friend and I reckon she doesn't always agree with her husband and has to try to keep him in order'.

Rebecca stayed in Canberra for the two months of that first sitting period of the Parliament. She then returned home to Townsville and tried to explain the mysteries of politics to some of her school friends. As an experiment, it could have had disastrous consequences for a youngster adjusting to family change but, in reality, it seemed to give her a boost in self-confidence. Having 'inside' information about her mother's new job gave her a special status and she continued to learn about politics, often travelling with me on weekends and spending holidays in Canberra.

Within a short time she was an 'expert' on parliamentary life and could rattle off details of marginal seats like a veteran. She later joined her school debating society and gave spirited defence of more controversial aspects of Federal Government policy. I used to worry that this constant focus on party politics might turn her into an apolitical adult totally disinterested in the democratic process, but she seemed to thrive on her early introduction to the political scene. I think our three children did become more politically aware because of their parents' participation, but they certainly developed their own strong convictions and did not necessarily agree with us. Indeed on many occasions there was vociferous family debate with me the only one defending the Labor Government.

Life in Canberra in those early months was most challenging. On one hand, there was the excitement of so much that was new – the place, the people, the protocols of the Parliament and, of course, the politics of a new government. The Hawke Government had swept into power with enthusiasm for fresh policy initiatives and an urgency for change. At the personal level, my predictable tropical lifestyle in a small city was totally overwhelmed by the demands on my life as a Queensland Senator.

In the Senate there were not only the rules of procedure to be followed but also some of the unwritten traditions to be adopted. It was expected that senators acknowledge the President of the Senate on entry and departure from the chamber. But what was the most appropriate way to conform? Some senators bowed low in a very formal way, while other gave a deferential nod of the head. The hushed atmosphere when I first spoke was in sharp contrast to the rowdy uproar of Question Time. I was allocated my own seat on the plush red-leather senate bench and found my desk drawer contained a personalised copy of Standing Orders. However, around the corridors in the Labor Party

Caucus Room, I had to join the rush to find a place in a room crowded with newly elected colleagues. Early in that first year, I took a central back seat, scarcely noticing that a few colleagues were looking on with some disapproval. I had occupied the very traditional place of dear Tom Uren, the Father of the House of Representatives, who had been sitting in the same place for over twenty years.

My office was tiny but overlooked the rose garden. At the start of each parliamentary sitting week, the gardener brought flowers for the 'lady senators', a tradition lost when we moved a few years later to the grand and very functional but impersonal new Parliament House. Parliamentary attendants appeared frequently to deliver mail and a range of parliamentary papers and reports. The paper war seemed impossible to manage as piles of publications cluttered the floor space waiting for me to decide which constituted essential reading.

Old Parliament House had a very friendly atmosphere because so many people were crowded together in a confined space. Offices were so small that we spent more time out in corridors, meeting rooms, the parliamentary dining room, the bar, the courtyard – even the toilets were places to meet and catch up on the latest gossip. King's Hall was located up a short flight of stairs from the entrance and its position made it a fascinating place because of the constant movement of people throughout. They congregated in groups to discuss the latest political drama. Corporate bosses and community activists waited for appointments with ministers or backbenchers. In those early months, Rebecca spent many hours 'people watching' in King's Hall, and on more than one occasion reported useful information about people she had seen talking there.

Life as a senator was complicated by the fact that I lived in Townsville, but had to work both in Canberra and around my large state. This involved hours of flying each week and a contrasting climate and lifestyle. I soon learned that the four hours travel to and from Canberra was useful for reading and drafting correspondence, speeches and press releases. One day, I sat with a colleague who was surprised that I was patiently opening all my mail on the journey home from Canberra. He said, 'Oh, you shouldn't have to do that – I just pack it in my suitcase and give it to the girls in the office!'

In Townsville, I had an electorate office with two staff, Penny Cook and Chris Hunter, both of whom had managed Jim Keeffe's office for several years. I was fortunate to move into an established order with experienced women who knew more about my role at first than I did. My days up North were filled to capacity with appointments, meetings and urgent phone calls. The mail that arrived was phenomenal: personal requests, general correspondence, party correspondence, demands for urgent action in every possible area of public policy, meeting agendas, parliamentary papers and reports from organisations and the business sector. Sorting correspondence according to priority was almost a full-time job and that was *before* we answered it. People came to talk about their individual problems with government departments – pensions, unemployment benefits and student allowances. Immigration applications and business schemes became very familiar as I learned to juggle half-hour appointments and resolve some of the crises affecting people's lives. I dutifully dictated letters to new ministers, urging them to get on with the job of overnight transformation.

After a few months, I realised that most of this ministerial correspondence was a waste of time in dealing with immediate needs. My letters disappeared into the black hole of the Canberra bureaucracy; only to be shuffled up and down the hierarchy for an often-indeterminate period of time before a response was finally returned to a minister's office for signature. Meanwhile, people were desperate for a resolution of their problems and had marched back to my office, thoroughly disgruntled that their newly elected senator had failed them.

I soon learnt to build personal links with local public servants who could resolve a number of issues caught up in the confusion of red tape so I reserved my direct approaches to ministerial offices for more complex problems. It was only as a last resort that I wrote to ministers on key policy issues where an individual circumstance revealed a hidden consequence of more arbitrary decision making.

In presenting my first speech to the Senate on 4 May 1983, I managed to weave into the text my commitment to social equity, feminism and Aboriginal land rights while, at the same time, highlighting the needs of rural and regional Queensland. It was to become the balancing act I tried to maintain throughout my sixteen years in Parliament, even though several 'advisers' told me to avoid controversy and to concentrate on the 'main game in town'. As a senator, I felt I had an obligation to both reflect *and* challenge community opinion, because I did not have the same constraints as a representative of a specific electorate.

This arrangement seemed to work well because I was able to complement the work of local members of Parliament, while continuing to advocate some more challenging reforms in regard to the rights of women and Indigenous people. I aimed to work at promoting the government's new initiatives as well as responding to local issues, which required some fresh vision. It was not necessarily the easiest course to follow and I did become embroiled in complex debates that attracted negative responses and criticism. Yet I believe the most important lesson I learned in attempting to deal with a plethora of demands from a diverse constituency was to act in accordance with personal conviction. Too frequently, the 'stage management' of political debate merely reinforces the scepticism that people have for their elected representatives. Most people, I found, were prepared to set aside areas of difference to concentrate on points of agreement that could produce a positive outcome. I didn't need opinion polls or spin doctors to tell me that Queenslanders expected to be taken seriously.

In that first year I travelled throughout Queensland, driving to coastal cities and towns or flying in small, chartered planes to remote communities in the west and far north of the state. Nobody knew me so I had to initiate these visits, inviting myself to local councils, industry groups, women's organisations and Labor Party branches. Gradually, I began to develop a reputation for being a representative of the state and was soon receiving invitations to attend a variety of events around Queensland. Even conservative communities appreciated that a voice in Canberra was more important than party politics, so I was able to build relationships with a variety of people more traditionally aligned to the National Party.

At the end of the year I compiled my first report to the electorate, in which I documented all my appointments for my first eight months in Parliament. I found my travel to and from Canberra, as well as all over Queensland, kept me out of my Townsville office more than I had expected and I heard whispers that people were complaining I was never there. I decided to put an advertisement in the local paper, detailing my itinerary each month so that people could see when I was available. It was an instant success and I maintained this practice throughout my parliamentary career.

CHAPTER 9

Women and politics 1984–1986

AFTER A FEW months, life as a Queensland Labor senator settled into an almost predictable pattern. I adjusted to the constant travel and alternate workplaces, learning to adapt my outfits to cope with both the icy winds of the south and the steamy blasts of hot air as I returned north.

In Canberra, I bought a red pantsuit, quite a respectable number I thought, until I wore it into the Senate and faced the disapproving glances of some colleagues and staff. Apparently, with so few women members, the wearing of such modern attire as pants had not been considered and I heard that such a precedent could be a breach of standing orders. Fortunately, President Doug McClelland was not so persuaded and the next day several women colleagues joined me in making this fashion statement, which twenty years on is considered standard dress for many women parliamentarians.

Parliament House became familiar, its corridors more easily negotiated as I learned to hurry from office to senate chamber and around the maze of committee meeting rooms. I loved the atmosphere of heightened expectation as decisions were taken, applauded or condemned while debate continued to justify or criticise policy directions. Whether in Parliament itself, at meetings with Labor colleagues or at senate committee meetings, the discussion could be either encouraging or dispiriting. On occasions, debate would move between the extremes of progressive and reactionary viewpoints, but the exchanges were never dull. There was always a follow-up challenge to either promote or counter a new policy initiative.

ACT Senator, Susan Ryan, had been appointed Labor's first woman minister. She was Minister Assisting the Prime Minister on the Status of Women and the office responsible was established in the Department of Prime Minister and Cabinet. This was an important signal that women's policy development would be a prime focus of the Hawke Government. Well-known feminist journalist, Anne Summers, was given the job of heading up this office to lead a transformation in policy reform. Many women throughout the national bureaucracy were ready to set in motion new opportunities for Australian women.

The positioning of the Minister Assisting, and the Office of the Status of Women, in the Prime Minister's Department was of both symbolic and practical benefit. Firstly, the profile of the status of women generally was raised, giving it the authority of the prime minister. And secondly, the opportunity for a close association with the cabinet process enabled new policy proposals to be monitored for their impact on women.

There had been an increase in the number of women members and senators elected as part of the Hawke Government. In the House of Representatives Wendy Fatin (WA), Jeanette McHugh (NSW) and Helen Mayer (Vic) joined Joan Child, the Speaker, Elaine Darling (Qld) and Ros Kelly (ACT) to increase the female representation. In the Senate, Ruth Coleman (WA), Pat Giles (WA), Jean Hearn (Tas) and Susan Ryan (ACT) were joined by

Olive Zakharow (Vic), Rosemary Crowley (SA) and me. It was a doubling of the number of women and we formed an influential in-house lobby as the Caucus Status of Women Committee.

The influence of this committee further strengthened the new administrative structures. The committee met weekly when Parliament was in session and had the authority to ask ministers and senior departmental staff to explain the progress of policy development and implementation. It was a powerful ally for the Minister Assisting the Prime Minister on the Status of Women, who could rely on her female colleagues when there were differences about policy direction or resource allocation.

We even arranged to 'shadow' our own ministers to monitor how receptive each was to the new reform agenda! Some ministers regarded us as mischievously interfering in their portfolio responsibilities but most accepted the advice of our committee. One high profile minister was guilty of referring to us as 'the old boilers', but later apologised. We also had the capacity to regularly ask senior departmental officers to address the committee and answer questions. Senior staff of the Defence Department, a particularly traditional hierarchy, were only slowly coming to terms with the new environment of gender equality. They arrived in uniform and nervously answered our queries about increasing women's participation in all areas of the armed services. We tried to be patient, but it was difficult to maintain our composure when most responses were prefaced by 'Now you ladies must try to understand . . .'

One of the most significant legislative reforms in the first term of the Hawke Government was the passing of the *Sex Discrimination Act 1984* to eliminate discrimination on the grounds of sex, marital status or pregnancy. This was a cause for much celebration among many Australian women who had been regarded as second-class citizens for so many years. However, it was also the subject of extreme hostility from more conservative sections of the community.

In Queensland I was responsible for communicating the benefits of this legislation, which would 'promote recognition and acceptance within the community on the principle of equality of men and women'. On one occasion I drove to a small country town in Western Queensland to present a speech to a large gathering of women vehemently opposed to the legislation. There were cat-calls and interjections of abuse during the speech, but the atmosphere improved during question time at the end of the afternoon. The one message that seemed to strike a chord of acceptance was my emphasis on the elimination of sexual harassment in the workplace. I related this to the daughters and granddaughters who might leave country areas and face harassment far from the security of home. It was a persuasive argument and by the time the meeting broke up for afternoon tea, I seemed to have at least a few supporters in the audience.

While there continued to be criticism of the *Sex Discrimination Act*, the *Public Service Reform Act* passed with less public antagonism. It required all Federal Government agencies to produce equal employment opportunity programs for four target groups: women, Aborigines and Torres Strait Islanders, people with disabilities and people of non-English-speaking backgrounds.

The Hawke Government had introduced the Community Employment Programme, which provided funding to local government to develop innovative employment creation schemes. I became an advocate for this program, persuading Queensland councils that it was not a wicked socialist plot as was often suggested by the state premier. Funding for these schemes required councils to adopt equal employment opportunity principles. A number of shire chairmen and their staff fumed about this dictatorial Canberra-based policy, which they insisted would not

Growing up in a quiet Tasmanian town in the 1950s was an unlikely introduction to a career in political activism. (Left, aged 12).

I needed little persuasion to join the ranks of the lively campus scene. Performing in the Uni revue, University of Tasmania (second from left).

A media shot for an article on Lachlan Park in the *Examiner* (1963). This period opened my eyes to discrimination and injustice. (Photo courtesy of the *Examiner*)

Henry and I at our wedding reception in Westbury, Tasmania (1963), just before we headed off overseas.

In Townsville in 1970, I was a regular visitor to the public gallery at Council meetings, but had to take John and Anna with me and try to concentrate while they played at my feet. One day two bored youngsters constantly interrupted me and finally John used his best stage whisper to demand a trip to the toilet . . . our presence seemed to encourage Council to transfer its meeting time to the evening.

My Council work in Townsville was very hands on. Digging for Telecom in 1979. (Photo courtesy of Newspix)

Taken at the launch of the Bicycle Safety campaign in Townsville in 1980. My Council work also had a strong community focus. (Photo of Rebecca and myself courtesy of Newspix)

A Townsville Labour Day march. Trade union support was central to my activism in Townsville during the Vietnam Moratorium. I had been part of the peace movement and had worked with the Townsville Trades and Labour Council over several years. (Photo courtesy of Newspix)

A photo with Henry, Anna and Rebecca in 1983 after I was preselected. (Photo courtesy of Newspix)

In 1987, I was elected into Hawke's cabinet as the Minister for Local Government. I much admired Susan Ryan's policy work as the Minister Assisting the Prime Minister on the Status of Women and when she left I was pleased to manage the portfolio.

Carmen Lawrence and I in 1994 launching *Herstory* at Parliament House. (Photo courtesy of AUSPIC)

A meeting of the Commonwealth Human Rights Advisory Commission, New Delhi, 1994. With delegates from India, South Africa and the UK.

Three generations of Reynolds women, Anna, myself and Jess, at the UN International Women's Conference in Beijing, September 1995.

I met UN Secretary General Kofi Annan as a delegate from Parliamentarians for Global Action (1997), pictured with others from Japan, Pakistan and India. (UN/DPI Photo by Evan Schneider)

Meeting with Madeleine Albright (former US Defence Secretary) at the UN in 1997. (see page 200)

Family Christmas in Tasmania, 2000.

work in the bush. They were, however, the first to boast several months later about the success of their local project, which had in fact employed large numbers of women and Indigenous people.

Meanwhile, I was preoccupied with defending the Labor Government's new policies, which were constantly being attacked by Joh Bjelke-Petersen. On one occasion I experienced an extraordinary incident in the Queensland Parliament. While visiting several Labor colleagues I was invited to attend Question Time and was shown into the Speaker's Gallery, reserved for official visitors. Soon after I was seated, the premier gestured in my direction and called out: 'What is the honourable lady, who is sitting there now, doing in relation to the defence of North Queensland?' He continued to ask me to justify myself in representing the state but, of course, as a visitor I had no right to reply. Amid an uproar of interjections and points of order, the Speaker gently rebuked the indefatigable Joh Bjelke-Petersen, reminding him of parliamentary protocol.

The incident reflected the determination of the premier to use every possible opportunity to confront the Hawke Government. In so many areas of public policy, which relied on constructive partnership between State and Federal Governments, the premier led vocal resistance, urging his ministers to ignore or attack any federal overtures that hinted at 'socialist reform'. The areas of conflict were predominantly in Aboriginal and environmental policy and industrial relations, though even routine issues within health, education, housing and employment created friction.

I was continuing my advocacy of regional policy because I found Federal Government Departments totally focused on capital cities. Whenever a new policy was announced I would scrutinise its effect on non-metropolitan areas and ask questions about its impact beyond the urban fringe. The Hawke Government promoted greater consultation with the general public but the bureaucracy's awareness of regional Queensland was limited, and some public servants seemed reluctant to take their public hearings into the depths of non-metropolitan Australia.

There was little understanding of distance or the scale of decentralisation in the sunshine state. On one occasion, I was amused to read a draft itinerary – planned in Canberra – which required a drive from Brisbane to Cairns (a distance of 1700 kilometres) in just two days, with several public hearings scheduled en route. On another occasion, my request for information on road funding included a city 500 kilometres south of the Queensland border. At the time I wrote in an electorate report:

> I have had some success in drawing attention to anomalies between capital cities and isolated regions. However I believe it will take years to re-educate southern bureaucrats and politicians about life beyond their comfortable lifestyle in the leafy suburbs of Canberra, Melbourne and Sydney – that magic triangle of decision making.

I may have started feeling secure in my new role as senator but, soon after my election, several of my Queensland colleagues were already plotting my political demise, determined that I would not succeed in the next preselection round to be held the following year. My fortuitous positioning in the 1983 election had not been forgotten (or forgiven), so ambitious men were preparing to force me into an unwinnable place on the Queensland senate ticket. There remained considerable resentment about my promotion by the National Executive from the obscurity of Townsville.

My situation was complicated by the fact that I was aligned to the Left faction in Canberra, but not all Queensland members of this group accepted me because I had failed to go through their processes. Meanwhile, Foreign Minister Bill Hayden hinted that maybe I could join his Centre-Left grouping, but I would have had to abandon my commitment to maintaining the ALP's anti-uranium policy, which was to be challenged at the next ALP National Conference.

In Federal Parliament I was seen to be aligned to the Left faction because of my focus on more progressive issues, but in Brisbane the Left had wanted the position for a long-serving trade union official. The two other factions wanted to guarantee the election of their chosen candidates, so I was very much out on my own. Ironically, when I personally approached the various key players in the ALP and trade union movement they all seemed to support the work I was doing. However I had moved beyond the standard processes of preselection, which meant I had to accept the consequences.

At the National Labor Women's conference in Adelaide in January 1984, North Queensland Aboriginal elder Thelma McEvoy demanded a unanimous resolution to ensure my re-endorsement. A few weeks later, Mackay member Wendy Trembath made a personal plea to Bob Hawke, who was visiting Brisbane. This exchange took place at the state ALP conference, where it was recorded by journalist Marion Smith who managed to secure a front-page story in the *Sunday Mail* headlined 'PM Pledges Support for Reynolds'.

For a few months there was considerable public debate and ongoing media comment. Many ALP branches and community organisations rallied to support me by sending letters to the prime minister, and it was obvious that my early months of working around Queensland had gained me a considerable level of support.

Finally, a deal was negotiated which resulted in the guaranteed preselection of sitting Senator Gerry Jones and me. While I could boast that my community support was responsible for defeating those rigid factional alliances, I should acknowledge the personal efforts and negotiating skills of Peter Beattie (then Queensland ALP Secretary) and Bob Hawke, who both worked hard to resolve the dispute in my favour.

Such preselection wrangles continue to mystify members of the general public, who are totally amazed that such energy and time can be wasted on these internal processes. It remains a challenge for modern parties to find a more open system for choosing parliamentary representatives. In retrospect I can now understand the uproar my original endorsement by the National Executive created, yet I know the preselection of a woman in those circumstances and at the time would have been impossible without that special intervention.

Over the next few years I managed to counter most of the hostility directed at me in that 1984 preselection. I worked hard to try to relate to the priorities across the factional system and to be proactive around trade union issues. I was myself a union member – firstly of the Queensland Teachers' Union and then the Queensland Nurses' Union when I was no longer employed as a teacher. I totally supported trade unionism as the foundation of the Australian Labor Party, but clearly on occasions there were tensions between my approach to some social issues and traditional trade unionism. I always tried to separate my feminist resentment of male power from personal relationships and generally was able to work well with a majority of Queensland trade union leaders, though I heard that several thought me to be both naïve and scheming.

The politics of Queensland continued to occupy a great deal of my attention. On 20 May 1985, fifty Queensland police officers stormed into the Greenslopes Fertility Control Clinic, interrogating its director, Dr Peter Bayliss, and demanding all medical records. Plumbers were called in to seal off street drains so police could gather evidence, and barriers were erected labelling the area 'Crime Scene Investigation'. Distressed patients and staff watched helplessly as women's files were removed and Dr Bayliss was escorted to a waiting police car. A smaller but equally disturbing operation was carried out in Townsville, where Dr David Grundmann conducted a similar clinic. By the end of the day, police had confiscated 47,000 personal medical records.

The Queensland Parliament had rejected legislation to outlaw abortion, a surprising victory given the dominance of the conservative National Party, not to mention the opposition of Catholics in the Queensland Labor Party. But the Right to Life anti-abortion lobby was both influential and persistent in continuing their lobbying for the closure of Dr Peter Bayliss's Greenslopes clinic. The Queensland Premier, Joh Bjelke-Petersen, said that the Attorney-General, Neville Harper, had the government's support in organising the raids: 'It was a cabinet decision to have the raids, yes, fully supported by the cabinet.'

There was a general community outcry about the gross breach of privacy and the way in which police had intimidated patients and staff. An opinion poll, commissioned by the *Courier Mail* and TVO Eyewitness News, found 77 per cent of women and 78 per cent of men disapproved of the raids, while 12 per cent approved and 11 per cent were undecided. The market research company, Frank Small and Associates, noted:

> Most people expressed disapproval of the raids and even disgust, especially at the invasion of women's privacy by the seizure of records. There is widespread outrage at the way the raids appeared to be handled even among people who personally are opposed to abortion. Some were surprised at the abortion clinics being raided at this time and concluded it was a government ploy to take attention away from other issues.

The Federal Labor Women's Caucus issued a press release calling on the premier to have all the records returned immediately to their respective owners, order the destruction of any copies made and apologise to all who had been so thoughtlessly and needlessly distressed.

In Question Time the day after the raids I asked Gareth Evans, as Minister representing the Commonwealth Attorney-General, to detail the civil rights of women whose private medical records were in the possession of police. He described the Queensland Government's action as: 'A graphic example of law enforcement going haywire ignoring the very values of personal liberty and privacy that the law and legal system is supposed to be established to protect'. He also said the issue was: 'An excellent illustration of the need for some overarching national civil liberty standards to be enacted for protection.'

In discussions with the Federal Human Rights and Equal Opportunity Commission I was advised that the action was in breach of the International Covenant on Civil and Political Rights, which states in Article 17:

> No one shall be subjected to arbitrary or unlawful interference with his/her privacy . . . and . . . everyone has the right to protection of the law against such interference and attacks.

It was probably my first opportunity to identify international human rights standards at the local level. As a result of the focus on privacy as a fundamental civil right the Attorney-General, Lionel Bowen, was urged to include a Commissioner for Privacy in drafting the Bill of Rights legislation.

During this period, my Townsville office became a central contact point for distressed local women anxious to understand the implications of their medical records being held for police enquiry. A number of women were fearful that family members would discover the truth about abortions organised independently. Some were so traumatised they were suicidal, but could not seek professional help because they considered that would further risk exposure.

My staff and I spent weeks advising and supporting women as well as being involved in mobilising women's organisations to demand a return of the medical files. It was a time when abortion law reform was on the public agenda and had overwhelming support. Around Queensland many angry women called meetings and organised a major state and national campaign for the return of individual files.

I not only wrote to the State Government, but also urged the Queensland Opposition Leader, Nev Warburton, to use this attack on women's rights to promote Labor's commitment to gender equality and freedom of choice. At a state council meeting he spoke strongly against the police raids and agreed to oppose anti-abortion legislation, which the State Government may have considered reintroducing.

However, there was such political uproar that the charges against Dr Bayliss were dropped and soon after a court ruled that the original search warrants used in the raids were invalid. Yet it was only a few months later that Peter Bayliss was charged again, this time with unlawfully procuring a miscarriage. He was acquitted when Judge McGuire ruled that the relevant section of the Queensland Criminal Code (Section 282) indicated that termination of a pregnancy was legal if it threatened the mother's physical or mental health. Technically, the Queensland Criminal Code had been interpreted in favour of women's reproductive rights, but legally the cloud of uncertainty remained.

By 1986, the Hawke Government was ready to introduce new legislation which continued the process of giving women greater opportunity in the work force. The *Affirmative Action (Equal Opportunity for Women) Act 1986* established the Affirmative Action Agency to oversee the requirement that all companies with more than 100 employees introduce measures and programs to attract and keep women in the work force. This policy was designed to change entrenched attitudes to women in the workplace and especially to encourage women to choose careers in non-traditional areas of work. Both private companies and universities were required to submit annual reports of the progress being made in implementing affirmative action. This policy was strongly resisted by a number of companies in the private sector and public criticism was vocal, with talkback radio hosts often encouraging extreme comment against women. There was also opposition within academic institutions, where just a small number of women had struggled for recognition and promotion. Both companies and universities were expected to report on their selection and promotion procedures as well as their progress in implementing maternity leave and work-based child care. There was ongoing dispute about whether the Affirmative Action Agency had any real authority to initiate reform, because the only penalty for companies which refused was to be named in Parliament.

Nevertheless, the overall impact of this legislation and the agency's work at that time was very important in changing attitudes to Australian women in the work force. By the time the affirmative action legislation was passed, Australian women's policy development was achieving international recognition as being both innovative and practical.

In particular, the adoption of a Women's Budget process requiring all government departments to report their progress was a major step in progressing reform. Each year a separate Women's Budget was produced as part of the Federal Budget. It detailed those initiatives and expenditure that had a specific impact on women. This focused the attention of both ministers and their departments and created an environment in which new policy could be developed. Obviously the process did not always deliver the positive outcomes that women wanted, but as a method for monitoring change it was very effective – so much so that it was adopted by many countries over the next ten years.

While there was considerable progress in implementing women's policy at Federal Government level, there was no action by the Queensland Government, which remained isolated from any progressive social reform. Little had changed since International Women's Year ten years earlier when there had been some modest legislative change to recognise women on an independent basis. The majority of other states complemented federal gender policy so I decided to document a comparative analysis to show the extent by which Queensland neglected policy to recognise women.

In January 1986, at a Brisbane press conference, I launched 'The Lost Decade for Queensland Women'. This document detailed all the Federal and State initiatives taken by governments since 1975 when International Women's Year had ensured some focus on women's policy. In releasing it I called on Queensland women to 'make 1986 the year that Queensland political parties are foced to listen to women's concerns. We can make a difference'. Researching the detail for my presentation I had discovered that Queensland had a comprehensive range of legislation about animals, as well as funded programs targeted at animal welfare, but nothing comparable which addressed the well being of women. In my speech I accused the Premier, Joh Bjelke-Peterson of caring more about animals than women. I must have struck a nerve because the Premier answered this allegation on radio saying if I continued to carry on like this I might lay an egg. I was delighted with his response as it precisely illustrated my message.

CHAPTER 10

Ministerial politics 1987–1990

After my re-election in 1987 there was the usual jockeying for ministerial promotion. In the Australian Labor Party ministers are selected first by their colleagues in the factions and then these choices are endorsed by a caucus meeting of all elected members and senators. Labor leaders then allocate ministerial portfolios to those individuals chosen by their colleagues, while Liberal leaders choose their own ministers independently. In 1987, two factors were influential in the decision-making process – gender and geography. Both issues were critical in my becoming a minister for the next three years.

On the Sunday after that federal election, the phone calls began from hopeful colleagues wanting my vote at a Left-faction meeting being held later in the week. Initially I had no expectation of nominating myself, because I was a relatively new senator with just four years experience and I knew there was fierce competition for the few available positions. However, I was determined that additional women should be included in the new ministry. Susan Ryan had been the sole female representative in the first two Hawke cabinets (1983–1987). In that time the Federal Government had prioritised sex discrimination and affirmative action legislation promoting the recognition of women in all aspects of Australian life. There was obviously an expectation that it was time the re-elected government increased the role of women in its decision-making processes. However, factional power rested with ambitious men who had majorities in all groups, so without specific intervention it seemed unlikely that women would be promoted. Indeed, at the time even Susan Ryan was at some risk, with murmurings within her Centre-Left faction that her position may not be secure.

I decided to speak publicly about the need for the factions to include at least one woman in their choice of ministerial candidates. I did so in good faith, but my motives were questioned because a number of my colleagues assumed I was pushing myself forward and interfering in factional processes which were not to be questioned. I had not intended that my advocacy for gender equality would translate into a personal opportunity as there were other women in my Left grouping who could well have claimed a ministerial position. Jeanette McHugh and Wendy Fatin both became ministers in the 1990s, but neither considered it timely to nominate in 1987 because that other issue – geography – was contributing to the debate about ministerial representation.

Bob Hawke had a problem creating some sense of balance between the states, as New South Wales and Victoria naturally dominated the vote in all factions, and therefore produced ministerial choices largely from those higher-populated states. Western Australia and South Australia were also well represented in the first two Hawke ministries, but Tasmania and Queensland had just one minister each. From 1983 to 1987, Bill Hayden, Minister for Foreign Affairs, had been Queensland's only representative in the federal cabinet. His portfolio responsibilities restricted the amount of time he could spend in his home state. It was vital for the Queensland Labor Party to increase ministerial representation, because that would enhance opportunities for challenging the Bjelke-Petersen Government.

At a state level, the ALP was gearing up for what was to become the Wayne Goss victory of 1989, and federal ministerial recognition was a very important factor in preparing that campaign. Furthermore, Queensland had contributed significantly to the 1987 federal election victory, winning four additional seats. The ALP had increased its vote throughout the state and, when preferences were distributed, the two-party vote was almost 50 per cent for Labor. Peter Beattie, then Queensland Labor Party Secretary, recognised the importance of this result as signalling the end of the Joh Bjelke-Peterson era and of the dominance of the National Party in Queensland. Bob Hawke also recognised the significance of the increased vote in Queensland, pointing out that: 'While we gained a little in other states, it was Queensland which contributed most to our increased majority'.

In the period immediately following the 1987 election, speculation grew about how the Prime Minister would reconcile these new demands to have a more inclusive ministry that reflected increased numbers of women and a greater recognition of the influence Queensland voters had on the election's outcome. Bob Hawke began a series of negotiations, making it clear publicly that he wanted more women and broader state representation in his revamped ministry.

Finally, despite serious misgiving about the power of the prime minister to impose his will on the factional system, both the Left and Centre-Left changed their original selection choices. Senator Bolkus and Senator Cook stepped aside to allow myself and Michael Tate (Tasmania) to come forward as the two people to satisfy regional interests. In addition, I joined Ros Kelly (Right) and Susan Ryan (Centre-Left) in demonstrating the factions' first commitment to gender equality. I was not popular for being a beneficiary of Bob Hawke's insistence that the factions recognise some electoral reality, but it did open up new thinking about the ministerial selection process. The *Age* reported: 'The Prime Minister yesterday got the Labor factions to bow completely to his wishes giving him a ministry containing three women, three Queenslanders and a Tasmanian.'

It was not the smoothest introduction to a ministerial position, with critics inside and outside the party predicting my early failure and sneering about 'that woman from Queensland' who just happened to be the only person qualified to combine those critical characteristics of gender and geography. I ignored the media's preoccupation with my situation until I finally responded to one persistent interviewer:

> There are bound to be questions of tokenism – token women, token Queenslanders, token Tasmanians, but if you like to turn the argument around, there have been a lot of token bloody men out there for a long time!

In fact, I was just the fourth Australian woman appointed to a national ministry position; as only Margaret Guilfoyle (Liberal) and Susan Ryan preceded Ros Kelly and me.

Although Australian women had won the right to vote in 1902, no women were elected to Federal Parliament until 1943 and ministerial responsibility was not offered to women for over thirty years until Margaret Guilfoyle became Minister for Social Security in the Fraser Government.

Choosing new staff to run my ministerial office was a difficult task in juggling competing needs. I wanted to employ people I knew and trusted, but I also needed specific expertise from staff who understood political, parliamentary and administrative processes. I chose Hazel Moir as my senior private secretary because she had an impressive background in public policy development, but she also won me over completely in the interview when she said she wanted the job because: 'Well, I figure not many women have ever been in your position and you will need someone like me to help you survive.'

She was right and her quiet combination of determination and assertiveness ensured that I managed to steer clear of any major political upheaval. Hazel knew I was vulnerable to criticism and so put considerable effort into establishing smooth procedures and good communication with departmental officers, colleagues, media and the general public.

I was appointed to the Local Government and Regional Development portfolio within the Department of Immigration, Local Government and Ethnic Affairs. My senior minister was Minister for Immigration, Mick Young, who provided this fatherly advice: 'Just keep your eye on the ball and stay out of trouble.' Other colleagues gave similar directives as I began work as a junior minister, but essentially I was free to set my own priorities providing I did not in any way bring discredit on the government.

One of my early decisions was to establish my ministerial office in Townsville and relocate my electorate office to Mt Isa. Members of the Canberra bureaucracy responsible for making this happen were aghast. How could a minister possibly function effectively from distant North Queensland and the even more remote mining town? And how would government business proceed smoothly without a Brisbane office to link in to that vast network in the Australian Capital Territory?

I had built my reputation on regional recognition, so was determined to try to put the rhetoric into practice. My ministerial position had been decided because I was a Queenslander, so it seemed logical to send a strong message about the location of my state headquarters. Decentralisation of government was of major importance to those two-thirds of Queenslanders who lived beyond the urban fringes of Brisbane. But in Canberra public servants were amazed that a minister would choose to locate so far from the centre of decision making.

However, I also had my political eye on that all-important 1989 state election, when Queenslanders would have the choice to change government for the first time in thirty-two years. I knew my decision would not only send a significant symbolic message, but would also provide a Labor presence in several state electorates.

Within weeks of my appointment I was placed in an acting ministerial capacity to represent Mick Young in cabinet. As he left for overseas commitments Mick gave just one instruction: 'Don't let those bastards touch my budget.' I was terrified I would fail him. How could I possibly argue against the Treasurer, Paul Keating, or Finance Minister, Peter Walsh, if they were to suggest 'rationalising' expenditure? Walking into the cabinet room for the first time was an overwhelming experience because my male colleagues had all sat together for four years, so knew the language and routine of national decision making. Unfortunately for me, neither Susan Ryan nor Ros Kelly was present that day so I entered feeling very isolated as the lone woman.

I expected serious analysis and discussion about the most effective strategy to be adopted. I assumed my colleagues would be thoughtful, as the weight of responsibility rested on their shoulders. I had sat up late into the night studying my cabinet papers and rehearsing arguments to protect Mick's budget should there be any assault from Treasury or Finance. I was prepared to be overwhelmed but impressed within this charged atmosphere of principled debate and allocation of the nation's resources. Instead

I found a noisy group of overgrown schoolboys jostling for attention and trying to outbid each other as the major carve-up of the 1987–88 Budget was finalised. Bob Hawke presided over this meeting with a calm demeanour of authority. I soon learned that when he lit a cigar it was the signal for argument to cease as he summed up the debate, nodded to a couple of protagonists and announced the general consensus to be recorded for posterity. Fortunately, the Immigration budget was not targeted that day so my first experience of cabinet passed without incident.

Not long after this meeting, I was phoned in my Townsville office by a senior Immigration official anxious to get my signature on a cabinet document. He insisted my attendance was unnecessary, but in the absence of Mick Young my authorisation was essential. The document was couriered north and I discovered a major policy paper. I phoned to check the status of the document because it had to be signed and returned immediately. I may have been a naïve new minister, but I was not prepared to sign a document I had not read.

The Canberra official was distinctly irritated and obviously worried the cabinet time frame may not be met because a nervous minister refused to accept his advice. Furthermore, there was the uncertainty about unfamiliar air-freight services from North Queensland to Canberra. I finally scrutinised this urgent cabinet paper and discovered some complex and far-reaching policy shifts in determining family reunion and working holiday visas. There was also comment on refugee policy which, at the time, meant little to me. However, it was clear that an attempt was being made to push through some significant policy shift changes while Mick Young was overseas.

I had no hesitation in signing beside the 'Not Approved' option, adding a note to the effect that this paper required the urgent attention of Minister Young before being submitted to cabinet.

Mysteriously, this paper seemed to disappear and, although I cannot now confirm all its policy directions, it appears likely that it did not surface in that form for several years. It was an important lesson for me in realising I had to use my own judgment as a new minister or I could find myself being used by a bureaucracy with its own agenda. It also demonstrated how easily bad policy can be pushed past a busy minister.

Life as a minister in those early months was marked by constant decision making. Not all decisions were momentous ones but people expected a minister to have an opinion on day-to-day functions of the office. Which policy? How many? Who to invite? When would an appointment be made? Where would an event take place? Some decisions required many hours of reading before final signature. There were decisions about routine procedures, staffing, new policy initiatives, inter-government protocols, political crises and of course the ongoing battle to secure funding. Everyone arriving in my office required me to make up my mind quickly so the wheels of government could roll on smoothly. But I wanted time – time to think and reflect on the best course of action, time to take advice from outside the inner circle of my staff and the bureaucracy.

I soon learned that ministers are time poor – every waking moment is scheduled and an army of inquisitors are programmed to demand instant attention. However, ministers are also protected to a large extent by solicitous staff who screen phone calls from overly demanding media or constituents. Staff become very protective of the minister and will spring to their defence when critics question whether policy or practice is being managed according to Westminster tradition. I was lucky to have a team of very supportive, capable staff who organised and briefed me, trying to put some order into the general chaos of a minister's life. Many critics of ministerial decision making have little understanding of the pace of life at the centre of government. It is assumed that ministers can make rational decisions based on reliable information and that a minister can always view all implications of those decisions into the future. Yet they often have to rely on the advice they receive from their bureaucracy and combine this with the demands of political agendas and the reality of public opinion. As a minister I wanted to set a reform agenda, but I soon found there were numerous constraints which forced me to tailor my expectations accordingly.

I had a young departmental adviser who was as helpful as he was charming. Although whenever I suggested a new approach to policy he would look very worried and say: 'Ah, but minister there is *danger* in what you say.' He would then proceed to list all the reasons why my idea was quite impossible to implement. I accepted some of his advice, but one day when he had again reminded me about the 'danger' of my proposal, I looked directly at him and said: 'Do you really think you are working with a dangerous woman?' He was confused, and for once did not have a ready answer, but he did not use that refrain again. We had a much more productive relationship thereafter.

I faced my first major political challenge when the Queensland National Party Government refused to accept a new national funding formula which offered greater predictability and equity in the annual distribution of revenue for Australian local councils. A major enquiry into the financial status of local government throughout the country had recommended major changes to the formula used for the Federal Financial Assistance Grants, which were paid to State Governments for allocation to councils. In Queensland, the Government had ensured that small rural councils were disproportionately advantaged compared with those larger urban councils on the coast, where National Party influence was less prevalent. Joh Bjelke-Petersen directed that the new formula was unacceptable because it was yet another sign of southern socialism imposing itself on the north.

I wanted to ensure that Queensland, of all states, would incorporate a fairer distribution of funds, and I also wanted to introduce the funding of Aboriginal councils. But the Premier was adamant he would not allow this level of interference from Canberra. Funding arrangements stalled and local councils began lobbying me to break the deadlock which had delayed funding. The fundamental principle of equity had been accepted by all other states, but the Queensland Premier thought change unnecessary and presumably recognised that it reduced his capacity to court favour with specific councils. Something had to be done to avoid conflict and disruption to funding, yet I did not want the Federal Government to capitulate to Joh Bjelke-Petersen.

I made an appointment to see Queensland Deputy Premier Russ Hinze, a larger than life character who was also responsible for Local Government, Police and the Racing Industry. Russ had a reputation as a no-nonsense trouble-shooter for the State Government, though some of his methods were definitely unorthodox. I knew him from my time with the Townsville City Council so I believed it was worth making a direct personal approach to find a solution to this inter-government impasse.

I arrived at Russ's office in the grand nineteenth-century Treasury Building in Brisbane accompanied by a personal staff member, Penny Cook, and a senior local government adviser, Rod Calvert. We were shown into the beautifully restored interior and found the Deputy Premier himself, a short and portly figure, draped on an elegant chaise longue beneath the window. As we approached to make polite greetings, Russ Hinze heaved himself into a sitting position, patted the rich red velvet upholstery and invited me to join him. 'Come and sit here with me, girlie,' he said in a friendly manner. For a moment I had no suitable response as Penny tried to contain her amusement and Rod shuffled papers to hide his embarrassment. Finally I managed to summon sufficient dignity to reply that we would be better able to have discussions if we all sat around a nearby table. Russ did not answer but left his splendid couch to preside over a formal meeting. During preliminary discussion I worried my rebuff may have disrupted resolution of our differences, but by the end of the meeting it was agreed that Russ Hinze would assure the Premier that the new funding formula would not disadvantage Queensland. In addition, Russ gave a commitment that the appropriate agreement would be signed immediately.

A second major Queensland issue to confront me within those early months in the ministry was the Federal Government's policy to end logging in North Queensland's rainforests. The spectacular area north of Innisfail to the Atherton Tableland and beyond to the Daintree River had been included on the World Heritage Register. This decision led to the creation of the North Queensland Wet Tropics Management Authority to monitor development in the region.

Prime responsibility for this federal policy rested with Environment Minister, Graham Richardson. However, several rural councils would be affected by the change to one of the major industries within their boundaries, so my department recommended a round of consultations to determine possible opportunities for alternative job generation in the region. We began organising to bring local councillors together to discuss the implications of Federal Government investment. As the locally-based minister it was my job to preside over several meetings where the resentment and anger of the local representatives was obvious. Nevertheless, we managed to negotiate our way through a range of potential new schemes with the aim of providing employment in tourism and related ventures.

Graham Richardson was not so fortunate when he visited the Atherton Tableland. Crowds of timber workers and their families blocked the road and buffeted his car, shouting abuse about the Federal Government's interference in the timber industry. Soon after this incident, a local school principal invited me to speak to his Grade 7 class about the role of government and its impact on the community. He wanted both sides of the logging debate presented in a learning environment, hopeful that it may ease the playground tensions caused by children articulating the views of their families.

I had no particular qualms about a debate with eleven year olds until I arrived at the school to find almost every family was in the audience for the occasion. This time I faced the antagonism of a community that would bear the brunt of the decision to end logging and close down the local industry. While I had campaigned for the World Heritage listing of the wet tropics and totally agreed with the merit of this decision, I could understand the views of individual families that had to adapt to new circumstances and unknown employment futures.

I began my usual lesson plan, dividing the class into 'Government' and 'Opposition' for a Question Time about local issues. Since 1983 I had developed a method of enabling school children to role-play parliamentary procedures to familiarise them with the way democracy functioned at national level. These lessons were always popular because the children chose issues they understood and were able to identify with a basic parliamentary process. Question Time in the classroom gave the opportunity for maximum participation and allowed children to dream up some very entertaining questions and answers.

On this occasion there was just one issue and all questions were dominated by criticism of my own government. The debate was lively, with parents cheering many of the responses given by budding young parliamentarians. Just a couple of children chose to defend the federal government decision and optimistically suggested that 'millions of tourists' would visit their town to see the rainforest. Despite the heated debate, the lesson ended with cheers for the performance of the Grade 7 students and we finished up the morning quite amicably.

Local government was a diverse portfolio which involved a great deal of travel throughout the country. At that time, there were over 800 councils and in three years I probably managed to visit only about one-third of them, including meetings where several councils came together for regional forums. While the image of local councils revolved around 'rates, rats, roads and rubbish', in reality there were many areas of public policy innovation which offered models of reform for State and Federal Governments.

Each year, my office organised a National Innovations Award with a variety of categories to showcase exceptional policy development in local government. Few of my ministerial colleagues regarded local government as very important in national policy terms, but in practice a local council could be involved in many areas of national policy debate, be it taxation or defence force training. Many councils in this period were committed to wide-ranging social policy initiatives in aged and child care, youth employment schemes, housing, and a range of cultural and recreational programs. I invited the prime minister to host annual consultations with local government representatives, and with several ministers in attendance, this one-day event started to build more recognition of local government as an equal partner with the states in national decision making and policy setting.

In 1990 I campaigned around Australia for acceptance of the referendum question that local government be recognised and incorporated into the Constitution. It was a popular issue within most urban and regional councils, though by the March election there was no national bipartisan support so the question was defeated. Of course the Australian Constitution is not renowned for being a reflection of modern Australia and reform via referendum is difficult. However, it is strange that the third sphere of government, democracy at the grass roots, is not acknowledged as such in our Constitution. The question put to the Australian electorate was a simple one: that local government be enshrined as a legitimate area of local administration. Nearly twenty years on, local government remains under-recognised as state and national bureaucracy assume superiority. Yet citizens are more likely to have a closer relationship with this sphere of government because both councillors and staff tend to have a better understanding of community needs than more distant state and federal representative administrations.

As Minister for Local Government, I was often the sole female in a variety of situations where it was assumed only men would normally participate. Since the late 1980s, Australian women have become much more visible as mayors, councillors and senior managers. However, in my experience, I found that local government culture was very much dominated by men and their priorities. In some states there was still resistance to a broader community-development role in local government. Those women breaking down barriers at this time found they were severely tested in attempting to raise issues of equal employment opportunity, child care and other proactive developments within social policy. I remember talking to a senior librarian who had considerable responsibility for several libraries and outreach services across the city. Yet she did not 'qualify' for a senior executive vehicle because these were reserved for the (male) engineers and accountants. When she queried this obvious lack of recognition, explaining it was difficult to fit boxes of library books in her personal small vehicle, she was curtly reminded, 'Well, nobody at

Council instructed you to deliver your books to nursing homes!' I don't imagine the fact that she also visited the prison would have enhanced her cause.

I tried to raise the profile of women in local government, arguing for new training options and the expansion of a scholarship scheme better suited to women. Towards the end of my term, I had a unique opportunity to consider women as candidates for appointment to head a major statutory authority. There was a vacancy for leadership of the Albury Wodonga Development Corporation, so lists of likely candidates were presented to me. These lists included a wide variety of male candidates, some of whom were distinctly ill-suited to the role, but not one woman's name appeared. I returned the lists to the Department, asking specifically for inclusion of some women candidates but was advised, with due seriousness, that this presented a major problem as there was no qualified woman available. I could not accept that in 1989 not a single Australian woman was regarded as sufficiently competent to take on this senior administrative role. I sought advice from some of my state colleagues in local government who nominated several women with appropriate credentials.

Finally, I selected Angela Munro, whose professional background and experience well suited her to the position. She became the first woman to head up a national statutory authority. I flew to Albury Wodonga to make the announcement and introduce her to the corporation. One junior staff member, a lively young woman, took me aside to congratulate me on my announcement. She giggled and confided that several of her male colleagues had been quite disparaging about a woman being appointed. Apparently they had joked about the arrival of the new Chief Executive Officer saying, 'No doubt the minister has appointed a girl with green hair and overalls!' Such was the attitude of some men to women in power.

As a minister, I was often asked to deputise for Bob Hawke at official functions in Queensland. In 1988, I was asked to represent the prime minister to welcome his Japanese counterpart to Brisbane, where the major Expo was being held. The protocol officer from the Department of Prime Minister and Cabinet phoned to give specific instructions about standard practice on such occasions and I was advised to arrive an hour in advance of the scheduled VIP flight. I presented myself at Brisbane Airport dressed in my smartest suit and was received by an obviously troubled official. He looked at me as if I was ill-prepared to take on this significant role as the acting prime minister. Had I chosen the wrong outfit for such an occasion or was my lipstick smeared? 'Where is your husband?' he demanded in an accusing tone. It had not occurred to me to advise that I would be performing this welcome *alone*. I apologised for my oversight, though I believed I should not have to explain that Henry had his own career and did not have to follow me around. Clearly a woman representing the head of state was unusual – and one without her partner seemed destined to create a diplomatic incident. Fortunately, the Queensland Premier's car was approaching, so the anxious supervisor of protocol rushed to greet him. Mike Ahern, Leader of the Queensland National Party, alighted from his white limousine and suddenly it was my turn to worry about official procedures. Mike Ahern was also alone – would that mean that the Australian welcoming party appeared as husband and wife?

The official party from Japan was almost due, so we were quickly shepherded to the red carpet on the tarmac. All proceeded smoothly as I was introduced to their Excellencies while Mike Ahern stood discreetly to one side awaiting his turn. Fortunately, he had not been mistaken for my husband, and no doubt he was equally relieved I had not been mistaken for his wife. After the formal greetings I escorted the honoured guests to the first of a fleet of limousines and then waited for my own car to join the motorcade into the city. I waited as cars, filled with Japanese staff and journalists, passed to join their leader. I seemed to have been stranded, yet the entire motorcade was dependent on my car's arrival as it could not leave without the Australian host. Protocol had stalled; there was no vehicle in sight and I was feeling decidedly foolish. Perhaps I should have brought my husband. Finally, my driver, Derek, signalled from a short distance away, revealing he had been blocked in by the number of over-enthusiastic visitors. I ran as best as I could to the waiting car, though my high heels limited my progress. I heard footsteps following me and reached the car just as a senior diplomat arrived at the same vehicle. He too was without transport, so had his eye on the sole remaining car. He graciously opened the rear door, offering me the back seat with his wife and secretary. Obviously he assumed his place was in the front. It was one of those occasions when I knew I had to assert myself on principle. After all, I reasoned, would a diplomat offer the back seat to the prime minister? Indeed, would he expect Bob Hawke to share the rear seating with two women?

I moved forward and put my hand on the front door handle and said firmly, 'I always sit in the front but you will all fit in the back.' I don't believe this particular individual was impressed with my display of feminist determination, but I felt this stance was warranted. The motorcade proceeded into Brisbane without further incident and I am confident our Japanese guests were unaware of the challenges to protocol during their arrival.

During my three-year term as Minister for Local Government, I also represented the Minister for Immigration in the Senate for my colleagues Mick Young and Clyde Holding, who were members of the House of Representatives. Senator Robert Ray took on this responsibility in 1989, but I maintained my role reviewing a certain number of individual ministerial appeals which had been rejected by the Immigration Review Tribunal.

My electorate office had always received a large number of requests for assistance with local immigration matters. Many enquiries involved requests for visas, especially for elderly parents, spouse sponsorship or extensions to working holiday visas. Together with social security queries, they constituted a significant volume of our constituent caseload.

Some of our appeals for more humane treatment had been successful, but a number were rejected by the Immigration Review Tribunal. I well remember the case of the British couple wanting to settle in Queensland, but despite their healthy financial situation and attractive work skills they were declined entry. The reason for this decision was traced to the fact that their family included a Down syndrome child who would require 'ongoing medical and institutional expenses', which would have to be met by the taxpayer and when the parents could no longer care for their child 'there would be an even greater expense on the public purse.'

Another case had involved over-zealous response to a character check for Australian citizenship, when an elderly resident was denied consideration because of a minor shoplifting offence. In one of a large number of cases affecting sponsorship of elderly relatives, a compliance officer threatened an incapacitated ninety year old, saying to her daughter: 'Madam, she will leave when the Department decrees and if necessary we will take her on a stretcher.'

However, this background did not prepare me for many of the heart-rending stories of appeal I would receive as a minister. Clearly I could not overturn all tribunal decisions, though some seemed unjustifiably harsh. I knew that departmental officers considered I took a 'soft' position in deciding some cases, so I tried to be rigorous in my judgment of very complex personal circumstances, many of which required a detailed understanding of global conflict and ethnic tensions. No doubt some of my decisions did not meet the approval of the Department of Immigration, but I always tried to balance my understanding of the legislation with recognition of personal circumstances.

Based on my reading of these immigration appeals, I believe the culture of the Department of Immigration was often less than generous, especially in those circumstances clouded by unfamiliarity and a degree of antipathy towards minority groups. Yet at the political level there was a fundamental commitment to a non-discriminatory immigration policy. One of the first signs of a breakdown in this bipartisan approach came when former Treasury head and new Queensland National Party Senator John Stone was elected. Senator Stone was critical of the government's selection policies, claiming non-English-speakers were not necessarily 'culturally compatible'. In April 1988, when I was answering a question about the long-standing bipartisan approach to immigration, Senator Stone interjected, suggesting he at least did not support this commitment. Following this exchange there emerged more vociferous political and academic debate questioning the extent of Asian immigration to Australia, which developed into the controversial policies articulated by Pauline Hanson nearly ten years later.

Living in North Queensland had alerted me to local racism evidenced on a daily basis by the treatment of Aborigines and Torres Strait Islanders, but I had not met specific hostility to Asians in North Queensland. However, during the 1988 debate about Asian immigration I woke in Townsville one Sunday morning to find our garage had been spray painted 'One Oz—No Abos—Asians Out!' It was obviously targeted at both Henry and me as we were both known for speaking out against racism. The culprits were never located but the incident did send government security monitors to re-evaluate our home and install new protective measures. I had never considered security a really serious issue until this time, when I realised the extent to which public life can attract critics prepared to take direct action.

CHAPTER 11

Changing politics 1987–1990

WHEN SUSAN RYAN retired late in 1987, her position was taken by Senator Peter Cook (WA) so I was asked by Bob Hawke to take on this additional portfolio of Minister Assisting the Prime Minister on the Status of Women. It was a job I welcomed as I had worked as a member of the Labor Women's Caucus and greatly admired all that Susan had achieved in the four years she held the position.

After several months as Minister for Local Government I was familiar with the key issues facing Australian local government and had adjusted to the day-to-day procedures of ministerial practice. I was very enthusiastic about having the opportunity to further develop women's policy but knew there remained major hurdles in maintaining the momentum for reform.

I was responsible for three offices, the central Status of Women office in Canberra and two women's information offices – one in Brisbane and the other in Hobart. By 1987, women's policy initiatives had been introduced by State Labor Governments in New South Wales, Victoria, South Australia and Western Australia. These administrations had appointed women ministers responsible for overseeing the work of specific women's units usually based within the structure of premier and cabinet. Similar equal opportunity and anti-discrimination legislation had been passed and a range of women's programs had been underway for several years. However, two conservative governments in Queensland and Tasmania had failed to introduce such women's policy, so the Federal Government had established the two women's information offices in Brisbane and Hobart to ensure women in those states at least had access to national women's programs. By the early 1990s, Labor governments in these states introduced their own women's policy units so these offices were absorbed into Queensland and Tasmanian state administrations.

My first task as Minister Assisting the Prime Minister on the Status of Women was to ensure cabinet approval of the National Agenda for Women. This comprehensive document was the government's response to the United Nations Forward Looking Strategies for Women consultations held around the country, where women had identified their key priorities for action. Twenty-five thousand women from diverse backgrounds had contributed to this process, which had created the blueprint for ongoing reform.

The National Agenda for Women listed the following areas of specific policy concern: consultation and participation in decision making, education, women at home and families, employment and training, child care, leisure, sexual discrimination, the portrayal of women in the media, social security, income security, superannuation, housing, violence against women and children, women with special needs, and international cooperation.

It highlighted the way government departments could lead reform which recognised Australian women as equal partners with men at home and in the work place. Fundamental to this was an expansion of educational opportunities for women. At the time statistics showed fewer girls stayed at school, went to university or studied science and maths. Women were still concentrated in secretarial, retail, nursing and teaching positions. We wanted to expand the horizons for young women as well as those returning to the work force.

The National Agenda was attempting to overcome the way women had been marginalised by incorporating an understanding of women's lives into policy. All areas of government had a responsibility to consider the impact on women of both policy development and the allocation of resources. Cabinet submissions would be required to have a comment from the Office of Status of Women. The idea that women were central to all policy development was a revolutionary idea for sections of the public service and indeed a few of my colleagues!

I knew there was some resistance within the ministry because certain men rejected new gender policy ideas as coming from middle class feminists, who did not represent working women. However, the history of Labor women reveals an ongoing struggle for equality within the working class movement of men determined to impose their priorities. I found women from many different backgrounds and age groups welcomed those policy shifts which recognised them and opened up new opportunities at home and in the work force.

I was quite confident about heading into cabinet to gain approval for the National Agenda for Women. I understood the full range of issues and the importance of getting every minister to accept responsibility for tangible change. I believed I could defend any objections. Only a few ministers questioned the policy paper, clearly concerned that women may exercise undue influence about resource allocation. However, Bob Hawke and others recognised that the National Agenda for Women demonstrated the government's ongoing commitment to policies which supported the changing role of women in Australian society. So the cabinet submission was approved and it became my job to promote and monitor its progress over the following two years of my ministerial term.

I found my role as Minister for the Status of Women much more demanding than I had anticipated. Policy reform in this area was still controversial and both the Opposition and the media were quick to seize on any opportunity to trivialise women's issues. I also received more than my fair share of hate mail and phone calls, usually from those who had personal reasons for being antagonistic towards social policy reform which benefited women. Some of the phone calls came from men who were angry about new family law and child support requirements, which placed more responsibility on fathers contributing financially to their children's wellbeing. Other correspondence revealed just how threatening a government policy shift seemed to certain individuals. A three-page letter I received from a critic highlights the challenge that feminist policy reformers faced in 1989:

> You and other radical feminists like Janine Haines are not only an embarrassment to this country but you are malicious trouble makers who just want GLOBAL FEMALE DOMINATION and I know you just want WAR with men. And lame duck organisations such as the EQUAL OPPORTUNITY TRIBUNAL, ANTI-DISCRIMINATION BOARD and FAMILY COURT should be dismantled and anyone like you who deliberately try to de-stabilise the country would be charged with SEDITION and imprisoned.

The depth of anger in such correspondence reminded me of some of the malicious letters and phone calls Henry and I received in Townsville about championing Aboriginal rights. It would have been easy to dismiss such criticism as the views of an extreme minority, yet there was clearly substantial resistance and misunderstanding about a reform agenda which merely articulated equality between men and women or between people of different ethnic backgrounds.

I always endeavoured to focus on equal power sharing and tried to highlight the benefits of working in partnership, but for some individuals the social shift was very threatening. On one occasion I was organising an International Women's Day event which was an opportunity to address a large and influential gathering of women. However, a male keynote speaker would not confirm his attendance and I was reliably informed by a member of staff that he had refused, saying: 'Tell them I am not going to be seen at that lesbian gang-bang.'

I often faced negative media where mostly male interviewers assumed that, as a feminist advocate for women's rights, I would automatically be a 'strident man-hating bitch'. On such occasions I tried to adopt my most 'lady-like' demeanour. I found that any mention of my husband and children immediately strengthened my position. I struggled with this conflict knowing that I should not be relying on marital status to argue my case, yet it was very hard to advocate basic reform from my position as an independent woman. I also realised that the most important aspect of my role was to advance rational debate for policy change, and if that necessitated compromise at this point, then perhaps it was justified.

To understand the position of Australian women at this time, it is important to reflect on our role in the work force. Between 1983 and 1987 there was a five per cent increase in women's participation rate, but our jobs were concentrated in two areas: community services and the retail trade. But legislative measures and government policy were slowly changing attitudes to women in the work place. The banking sector was one of the first to change, employing women at more senior levels and in 1987 the State Bank of Victoria announced its decision to extend maternity leave from twelve to eighteen months.

In 1989 the women's magazine *Portfolio* reported:

> Women in the paid working landscape have been a major feature of Australian life for only the past twenty-five years. But in spite of our relatively recent arrival, women are making enormous inroads into the middle echelons of business and are having an increasing impact on upper management.

In its article, 'Women of Influence', thirty-four women were identified, many being the first to occupy senior positions in government, unions or the private sector. Senator Janine Haines (Democrat) was listed as the first woman to head a political party. The Defence Department reported that Pageen Mallan was the first woman to become a Group Captain in the RAAF in July 1983 and the most senior army officer was Colonel Janice McCarthy, promoted in January 1988. The Australian Navy identified two female Commanders, Patricia Downs and Helen Marks. Mary Gaudron had been appointed the first female High Court judge in 1987 and Jane Mathews was the first woman to become a crown prosecutor in New South Wales.

Only one woman, Helen Williams, had attained the level of Associate Secretary (Transport) within the federal public service. Jennie George was an impressive pioneer, being the first woman to head both the New South Wales Teachers' Federation (1980) and the Australian Teachers' Federation (1985). In addition she was the first woman to be a member of the Australian Council of Trade Unions (1983) and its first woman vice-president (1985). Two women, Sally-Anne Atkinson and

Winsome McCaughey, were leaders in local government – Lord Mayors of Brisbane and Melbourne. Other women named represented achievement in the arts, science, sport, advertising and publishing, but there was a notable absence of women leaders in Federal and State Governments, tertiary institutions, medicine and major companies.

While the acceptance of principles of affirmative action and the pace of change was slow, the National Agenda for Women was starting to be implemented by a number of my cabinet colleagues, who had begun to take some pride in what their departments were doing to promote gender equality.

Gareth Evans, Minister for Foreign Affairs, had promoted several women to senior diplomatic postings and AusAid introduced a specific 'Women in Development' program, recognising that funding projects that focused on women's role in community life was central to the country's overall economic and social progress. In the Defence portfolio, Kim Beazley presided over a department which had, in five years, increased the percentage of Defence Force positions open to women from 8 per cent to 35 per cent. The first women pilot trainees had entered the Air Force in 1987 and there was a significant expansion in the number of trade-based positions and apprenticeships open to women. In his opening address to the Women's Tax Convention in Parliament House on 4 March 1989, Minister for Primary Industries and Energy, John Kerin, recognised the importance of women's priorities in the key debates about wages and taxations.

The role of Bob Hawke as Prime Minister overseeing the most radical reform agenda for Australian women has not been fully analysed, but his leadership and support between 1983 and 1991 were fundamental in enabling Australia to become an international leader in gender policy development. For many people familiar with Bob's personal and trade union background he was an unlikely advocate for women's equality. In his own family Hazel had forgone her career to accept full responsibility for child rearing and home management, so Bob enjoyed the luxury of focusing on his role as trade union leader, politician and ultimately prime minister. He had developed a reputation as a typical Aussie male, so it was unexpected that his role would be crucial in initiating such a period of change for Australian women.

Initially, I had certainly had doubts about Bob's support for developing women's policy initiatives. But his trade union background actually gave him an understanding of the pressures on low-paid women workers, and he recognised that something had to be done to increase Labor's share of the women's vote through representation. No doubt much credit for influencing Bob Hawke's attitudes on women's rights must go to Hazel and their two daughters, who articulated strong feminist principles.

While working with Bob, I found he had a genuine belief in advancing opportunities for women and was personally committed to legislative and administrative reform to guarantee that progress was made. In cabinet he cut short any debate that reflected a more traditional view of women's roles, and urged his colleagues to push ahead with the reform process. Of course, this did not always guarantee that specific policies were fast-tracked, but from my observations this was always a clear expectation of the prime minister.

At a personal level Bob was receptive to new ideas though it was not always easy to get his attention and I seriously questioned whether taking up golf would give me more opportunity for discussion. Nevertheless he was usually quick to respond and I could not fault his capacity for being fair and open-minded about several controversial debates, which a less secure leader may have tried to cut short.

He was particularly supportive of two campaigns launched during my term as minister. The Portrayal of Women in Advertising and the National Domestic Violence campaigns had been identified by Australian women as priorities for government action during the nationwide consultations held to develop the National Agenda for Women. Both campaigns were based on challenging stereotypes about women's place in Australian society, and both had the potential to attract criticism because neither had previously been considered the concern of government.

Gaining final approval for the first national advertising campaign to raise awareness about the extent of criminal assault against women was a fascinating exercise in sexual politics. A comprehensive media campaign had the general agreement of cabinet, but I had to present the detail to a specific subcommittee for final approval. I was nervous about the all-male reception to some of the content, which was quite confronting. The research had revealed one in four women had experienced some form of domestic violence and a community attitudes survey revealed an alarming acceptance that men had a 'right' to discipline their wives in certain circumstances. I wondered how some of my colleagues would react to this campaign which focused on individual behaviour within the private domain of family life.

The television advertising bookings had been made and we had a date for the launch of this important public awareness campaign. However, there had been a delay in scheduling a meeting of the cabinet subcommittee. Finally a date was set but it coincided with a parallel commitment I had in Wollongong, where I was due to announce the 1988 Local Government Innovations Awards.

I had advised the chairman of this subcommittee that I would like my item brought forward on the agenda because I had to leave Canberra early when Parliament was still sitting. The meeting started on schedule, but was interrupted by an urgent request for a minister to return to the senate for half an hour. It was not my portfolio so I was surprised to be asked to go back to the chamber instead of presenting details of the national domestic violence advertising campaign. I protested that I had a tight schedule to get to another appointment. The chairman said the domestic violence submission could be done quickly but *after* I returned from doing some duty in the Senate chamber. Again I argued my particular time pressure that afternoon. There was silence and six male colleagues looked at me expectantly. I knew I had no choice. No one spoke, but I recognised that if I wanted my submission agreed to expeditiously, I had to accept the decision of the majority. So I dutifully went back into the Senate and when I returned with only minutes to spare, my smiling colleagues advised they had approved my submission. I had been rewarded for complying with their wishes and the detail of my submission was almost irrelevant. These kinds of situations were annoying, but I learnt to be pragmatic as I knew it was counterproductive to challenge this show of male authority at such times.

In the lead-up to a national forum on the Portrayal of Women in Advertising, held in Sydney on 13–14 October 1988, a study was conducted to assess how women were being stereotyped in television, radio and print advertising in areas like occupation and behaviour as well as sexual references.

Many of the results were entirely predictable in reinforcing that women were overwhelmingly portrayed in family settings and supportive roles. Women were used primarily to advertise personal care, food and cleaning products and were rarely seen as authorities on any subject. Sexual references dominated and one in seven advertisements showed scantily clad women, while one in ten exploited sex to promote the product. In the print media there was a disproportionate preoccupation with women's appearance, and men were more likely to be shown in active roles, while women were more likely to be depicted in submissive positions.

The Portrayal of Women in Advertising Forum attracted over 500 participants representing government, the advertising industry and women. There was obvious polarisation in many of the views expressed, with one representative of the Advertising Federation of Australia claiming that the forum was 'wasteful and creating discord where none existed.' Yet guest speakers from Canada and New Zealand said the Australian research paralleled their own and that specific government intervention was necessary to control the sector. Quentin Bryce, the Sex Discrimination Commissioner, suggested that this legislation could be amended to include sexist advertising as a form of discrimination. During the two-day debate it was instructive to watch the way in which women from vastly different backgrounds came together to demand change. Young women with outspoken views liaised with their more cautious elders, and were able to present government and industry with a united voice which detailed a program for change. As a result of the forum, a National Working Party on Women in the Media and a Media Watch organisation were established.

During the next few years, women's policy development in Australia became fairly well integrated across all Federal Government Departments. However, I did find that when new initiatives were being announced my male colleagues were keen to be in the limelight, but when ever there was a negative public debate about some aspect of women's policy then it was up to me to explain.

Part of my ministerial responsibilities required me to visit other countries in the region which gave me an opportunity to compare policy and practice with my ministerial counterparts in other places such as New Zealand, Japan and the Philippines. This was my first real experience of the support that can be obtained and given through international networks of women.

In 1989, I visited Margaret Shields in New Zealand, who headed the Department of Women's and Maori Affairs. New Zealand and Australia had a friendly rivalry about our respective policy initiatives to upgrade the status of women. We shared the same commitment for change but had different approaches. New Zealand had chosen a specific women's ministry model arguing that Australia's mainstreamed approach within the Department of Prime Minister and Cabinet did not provide the focus guaranteed by a separate department. My colleague was proud of her portfolio achievements, yet constantly battled the bureaucratic processes to prevent her newly established department being sidelined. On the other hand, I enjoyed the apparent 'luxury' of being based within the most influential government department, but had to try to keep up with all departments' agendas.

Both models have their advantages and disadvantages, but I would opt for the more integrated approach providing there is strong leadership at prime ministerial level. To a certain extent I was disadvantaged by not having cabinet status like my New Zealand colleague. While I could always attend any cabinet meeting where gender impact was likely to be debated, I remained junior in status so could not always succeed in promoting specific policies.

In 1990, as part of my ministerial responsibilities, I also visited Japan where I met Chief Cabinet Secretary Mayumi Moriyama and Minister of State Sumiki Takahara who were eager to compare notes about women's representation in Parliament, as there had been a recent increase in the number of women elected to the Japanese Upper House. They were impressed to hear that in Australia in 1990 women made up 22 per cent of the Senate, but, as in Japan, numbers in the Lower House were considerably less.

During various exchanges with Japanese representatives of the League of Women Voters I heard a great deal about campaigns opposing the consumption tax and any change to the country's non-aggression pact. They were also vehemently committed to raising the profile and influence of Japanese women. One recently elected young woman described her first parliamentary speech in graphic terms:

> When I began speaking there was so much noise and laughter so I said one day you will see many women here with me. One man shouted back – 'If that ever happens I will vomit.'

As well as focusing on women's policy and the progress being made by the Japanese Government in implementing the United Nations Forward Looking Strategies for Women, I met with senior local government officials about a range of issues including direct flights between Australia and the Kansai International Airport, which had the potential to reduce flying time to six and a half hours between North Australia and Southern Japan. In Ikeda City I was invited to participate in an annual 'Coming of Age' ceremony. This invitation owed much to the fact that Ikeda has a long-standing sister city relationship with my home city of Launceston, Tasmania, so councillors were pleased to have a guest speaker who had been born and educated there. 'Coming of Age' ceremonies are very colourful and impressive occasions because they feature young people's entry into the adult world. The women wear beautiful traditional kimonos and the men formal suits. It is a ceremony that honours the city's youth and welcomes them as citizens.

It was my visit to the Philippines as an Australian Government representative that really opened my eyes to Australia's global responsibilities on human rights. Our visit to Manila was during a time of heightened political tension in the Philippines. Only days before we left Australia, the Department of Foreign Affairs advised cancellation because of uncertainty about political demonstrations. However, the itinerary had been organised and I had several major commitments to discuss the issue of Filipino brides as Australian migrants, so we proceeded with the visit. The drive through the streets of Manila shocked me because the poverty was just so stark. I found the situation of street children and adult beggars especially confronting. It was not my first visit to a developing country, but there seemed a greater level of despair and deprivation than I had seen in the 1960s. Perhaps it was in part the contrast with my own situation. As I sat in the ambassadorial limousine being driven to the comforts of a first-class hotel, small children pressed their sad faces up against the car windows, their eyes downcast as they pleaded for a few coins that might provide a little sustenance. But the windows had to remain firmly shut as we were told any offering would cause a stampede in these overcrowded streets where so many were in need. My official escorts waved the children aside and the driver blasted the horn so everyone scattered as the car gained speed.

In the Philippines I found it difficult to relax and enjoy the new culture. I found the extremes of wealth and poverty disturbing, more so because as an official guest I was treated to quality accommodation and meals. The suburban compounds, gated and patrolled by armed security guards, were an ongoing reminder of the extreme divisions in this society.

One of my priorities in visiting Manila was to make contact with government and women's organisations about protecting local women who were exploited as 'mail order brides'. There were some serious concerns about the ethics of certain agencies which exploited these women and a number of Australian men were engaging in serial sponsorship. Some Filipinas experienced extreme isolation in rural communities with men who were violent and controlled their wives by threatening to have their visas cancelled. Others were forced into prostitution by their fear of being deported. In addition, at the time a local tourist agency openly promoted sex tours attracting Australian men to take advantage of prostitution involving very young girls. On my flight into Manila it appeared more than coincidental that there were so many groups of middle aged men apparently on an overseas jaunt for cheap sex. Both government and church non government organisations were extremely vocal about the failure of the Australian Government to take any responsibility for the behaviour of some individuals who exploited the poverty of young Filipinas. In these official consultations I assured staff that I would make recommendations to the Prime Minister to try to overcome the exploitation of so many young women.

On the second day of our visit our itinerary included an official luncheon followed by a visit to an AusAid project in the area of 'Smokey Mountain', renowned as a large inner-urban slum of thousands of families struggling for survival. My private secretary Frances and discussed the dilemma we faced in knowing what to wear for two such contrasting commitments. To dress casually for a formal luncheon would have been an insult to our hosts, yet we had to consider our second appointment. We compromised by taking a change of shoes and removing jackets and jewellery to minimise the possibility of looking like arrogant, privileged westerners. The luncheon was magnificent and was held in the elegant colonial hotel, which was General Macarthur's headquarters during World War 2. Then it was just a short journey to another part of the city where we visited the women's development project funded by the Australian Government.

We were led by diplomatic staff through a maze of shanties and along narrow planks, which formed bridges across open sewers. The stench was nauseating and the hostile stares of many people hunched in doorways made me feel extremely uncomfortable. Was it appropriate to be prying into the lives of these people? We finally reached the tiny hovel where twelve women were tightly wedged, each seated at a sewing machine. Introductions were made and translated but our presence was scarcely noted as the women continued stitching, their heads bowed over coloured cloth.

Conversation was stilted until I asked about several hand-drawn posters displayed along one wall. These contained images of women and children in front of a barbed wire fence patrolled by soldiers. I could not read the text so gestured towards the posters, requesting a translation. My interest in the posters had an immediate effect on the sewing group. Women began to speak with great animation and our interpreter could scarcely keep up with the several voices anxious to communicate. Stories of prostitution, rape and violence emerged as anxious officials proceeded to move on the ministerial party. That sewing group included vocal opponents of American bases in the Philippines. As we left, one woman insisted on giving me a photo of a young boy shot while foraging for food near the United States military base. I subsequently made further enquiries about the allegation, but it was dismissed as fabrication. I well remember the agonised expression on that woman's face and believe she spoke from deeply personal knowledge.

I made a full report to Bob Hawke focusing mainly on issues affecting women in the Asia Pacific region. Initially, when I had raised my concerns about the treatment of Filipina brides, my Department had assured me there was nothing that could be done in the area of private behaviour between consenting adults. However, the Australian Embassy in Manila began to offer special pre-marriage counselling to couples and there was greater understanding within the Department about the vulnerability of women dependent on former partners for valid visas. Furthermore, within the Department of Foreign Affairs there was growing concern that the behaviour of some male tourists in South East Asia was reflecting badly on Australia generally. I maintained links with a number of international organisations campaigning to control the behaviour of westerners engaged in child prostitution. A few years later Federal legislation was passed to prosecute Australian citizens involved in sexual offences while travelling overseas. On its South East Asian flights Qantas introduced the distribution of pamphlets detailing the criminal nature of such behaviour and the Federal Police set up a unit to monitor the impact of legislation in Manila and Bangkok.

After the 1990 election, I decided not to recontest a position in the ministry. I had been involved in a car accident while inspecting damage after a cyclone and experienced spasmodic back pain for several months. I also knew that only one woman from the Left faction would succeed because so many of our male colleagues assumed it was their right to be promoted. I reasoned that I had enjoyed a three-year term as minister and it was time to move aside for my friend and colleague, Wendy Fatin.

I think too many ministers are overwhelmed by their responsibilities and lose touch with their communities while totally relying on public servants to brief them. In my view we need to 'rest and revive' our ministers, rotating responsibility so that there is a fresh approach and more thorough oversight of departmental practice. At the same time the role of backbench members is vital in monitoring the performance of ministers and their departments. In an ideal world more ministers would have the opportunity to step aside from their portfolios, regenerate and return afresh, but I see little prospect of this in the harsh and competitive environment of politics. Unfortunately, when ministers move to the backbench it is usually seen as a demotion and some individuals cannot imagine remaining in the parliament after they have left ministerial office. Yet those who do decide to remain on the backbench can make an outstanding contribution because they understand how government really operates from the inside. These skills are essential in opposition but are also important in all aspects of parliamentary and committee work, from estimates committees to international diplomacy. I had thoroughly enjoyed the challenges of my three years as a minister but I was ready to return to a more personal 'grassroots politics' and to use the knowledge I had gained as a minister both in Australia and overseas.

After leaving the ministry I wanted to continue promoting women's rights and to continue to expand my interest in women's rights internationally. As a minister I had the opportunity to travel and meet women from other cultures, so I wanted to continue working to better understand the global women's movement. My first opportunity came soon after the 1990 election, when I was invited by Zoya Pukhova, President of the Soviet Women's Peace Committee, to visit Moscow to participate in a special event to mark the tragedy of Chernobyl. In 1986, an explosion and fire at the Chernobyl Nuclear Power Station had caused widespread death and destruction, with ongoing severe medical impacts for many Russian citizens. I had met Zoya when she visited Australia the previous year to study our women's policy initiatives. The Soviet Women's Peace Committee was an influential national organisation which was working to assist the rehabilitation of many women and children affected by the Chernobyl disaster. They raised money and used their international links in the women's peace movement to publicise the need for medical research and support for the victims. My secretary, Penny Cook, and I were welcomed as guests and hosted by this women's organisation for ten days in May 1990. I was greeted at the airport by women carrying red carnations, the Soviet symbol of love for the sons who have died in war.

My first commitment was to participate in the Chernobyl 24 Hour Television Marathon to raise funds for the victims of the nuclear disaster. The event was transmitted by satellite around the world and many countries were represented at the solemn opening ceremony, which was addressed by a woman who survived the bombing of Hiroshima. I presented a donation from the Australian Government and a message from Minister for Foreign Affairs, Gareth Evans. I was also able to give several donations from local organisations, including the Women's International League for Peace and Freedom and People for Nuclear Disarmament. The crowds were quite overwhelming, with people pushing forward to give their personal support, and the speeches continued overnight as people from around the world gave their support. In the foyer there was a photographic exhibition of the disaster, showing horrific images of so many people, especially children, who had been grossly disfigured. Many doctors were present to explain the treatments being utilised and to detail the health impacts on Soviet citizens. At the time, it was estimated that many thousands of children had been affected and a large number were not expected to live beyond their fifteenth birthday.

In Moscow, we spent two days in discussions with women's organisations and representatives from the Department for Women's Issues and the USSR Council of Ministers. Many issues discussed paralleled women's concerns in Australia, with child care being the top priority. I was interested to hear negative comment about family planning on the basis that, after all, the

Soviet needed more citizens and every woman hoped to produce another Yuri Gagarin (the first Soviet citizen to successfully fly into space). We also sat in a debate at the Kremlin and, although we could not follow the proceedings, our interpreter told us it was the final stages of the Pensions Bill, which was not passed that day because of lack of a quorum.

On 1 May, Penny and I watched the thousands who marched into Red Square carrying garlands of flowers, placards, balloons and flags for the traditional workers' celebration. The square was dominated by huge May Day posters of Soviet heroes – Marx, Trotsky and Lenin – and red flags flew from many buildings and lamp posts. Our seats gave us an excellent view of the marchers as they approached the small incline near the Kremlin. It was an amazing spectacle. There were cheers and calls of 'perestroika', which recognised Gorbachev's efforts in economic reform as well as his leadership in committing to a peace dialogue with the United States. The themes of the speeches revolved around living standards, the environment and peace, with one banner proclaiming in English 'Moscow needs clean air.' Only one woman worker spoke and she congratulated the organisers on the new style of celebrating May Day, which for the first time did not include a display of the Soviet military machine. She received rousing applause for her statement, 'This year we are not boasting about our preparations for war'. Mrs Gorbachev walked past our stand with her granddaughter and Gorbachev himself was on the podium at Lenin's Mausoleum, just beside the main gates into the Kremlin.

During our time in Moscow we visited several magnificent ornate Russian Orthodox churches characterised by many large frescoes and mosaics. At one we met the charismatic Father Viktor who invited us to share his evening meal, which turned out to be an impressive spread of food and wine left over from his lunch with the bishop. We had a most entertaining hour discussing the meaning of life and whether all Australians were 'believers'. He proposed a toast to Love – spiritual, of course, he said with a wink – and he concluded by singing prayers in a rich baritone voice. As we left he insisted on giving each of the five women in our party 'kisses of Easter'.

At the weekend, we travelled overnight by train to Leningrad and were met by three women veterans – Anna, Katherine and Irina – who had each survived the World War 2 siege of their city. When Hitler isolated Leningrad for 900 days in 1944, one and a half million people died of cold or starvation. Anna, at sixteen, had buried thirteen family members in mass graves, carting their bodies week after week on a small sledge she had previously used for play. We visited the massive area of war graves at the Piskarevsky Memorial where we walked in the rain listening to the haunting sound of Shostakovich's *7th Symphony* playing continuously in tribute to the heroes of Leningrad. During our stay in this amazing city of such endurance, we also explored the history and culture of the vast collections in the Hermitage Art Museum and the magnificent country retreat of Catherine the Great at Pushkin. Catherine's Summer Palace was occupied by German troops who damaged much of the interior, but 'before and after' photographs showed the success of meticulous restoration. At night we were taken to the opera *Boris Godunov* at the Kiev Theatre. Throughout our visit we were treated to wonderful hospitality, yet we recognised that our experience was not shared by most Soviet citizens. In all our meetings, men and women reminded us how much better Russian society would be when they had a market economy. Our interpreter, Helena, though, revealed her doubts about the impact of change on their society, saying: 'What purpose of a revolution if we are to give it all away?'

Returning to Australia I was interviewed by a local journalist who headed his story 'Senator Reynolds impressed with Soviet society and culture'. In the interview I was able to speak about the positive aspects of Soviet social welfare commitments to women, including three years maternity leave for mothers and, where necessary, even grandmothers. However several irate constituents phoned or wrote to me and were very critical of me 'wasting money on talking to communists'!

Later that year, Henry and I travelled to South America with the Parliamentary Delegation attending the International Parliamentary Union (IPU) Conference in Uruguay. It was an important opportunity to discuss women's political representation in a large number of countries and to lobby for the IPU to commission a study of progress being made in the election of women. The IPU was very much a male bastion, with a number of men genuinely surprised that there were women attending who wanted to see an increase in their number. Kathy Sullivan, Member for Moncrieff, and I were both Australian representatives on the delegation so we worked together to get gender issues debated. We set up a small, informal women's caucus representative of mainly European countries, Japan, India, Cameroon and Canada.

At our conference, only nineteen per cent of the delegates were women so we lobbied to have the IPU adopt policy for better representation of women, and surprised the final session of the conference by seeking leave to put forward a resolution calling for all member countries to increase the participation of women. The Chairman was obviously nervous about such a move and several male speakers pointed out that we had not gone through the proper procedures for resolutions to be presented. As it was an all male committee we had assumed this might be a waste of time. Nevertheless we had a spirited debate and a few years later it was apparent that some improvement in women's participation was underway.

After that conference, Henry and I flew to Chile, where an official itinerary had been organised for me. I met with a range of human rights groups and women's organisations. I was briefed on the post-Pinochet environment and the gradual return to democracy after the years of terror under the military junta. I attended a wonderful ceremony in a poor community on the outskirts of Santiago where women were celebrating their first vote in local elections. It certainly reminded me how cavalier we Australians can be about our democratic freedoms. There, in that shanty town, women of all ages had dressed up for the special occasion. There were speeches and music and dancing to mark their achievement and through my interpreter, I heard the level of commitment they articulated about being privileged to vote. This was such a sharp contrast to the way some Australians complain about compulsory voting.

My most memorable visit in Santiago was to the San Domingo Prison, where I spent several hours with women political prisoners still detained for alleged crimes during the Pinochet regime. It had not been easy for the Australian Embassy to get permission for our visit but finally a staff member, an interpreter and I were driven to the stark entrance of that notorious prison. I found the obligatory search and removal of all my personal possessions very intimidating. There was no doubt that prison officers resented this official Australian visitor and wanted to remind me I would be treated exactly the same as the locals. However, once inside I soon forgot about my introduction to the prison because I met the most inspiring group of women. They had created an extraordinary living environment within the walls of that gaol with colourful paintings and craft work that disguised the drab interior. They had made a garden in the courtyard and were just finalising the printing of their weekly newsletter which was sent out to their families and women's groups. I was amazed by the general atmosphere which was so vibrant with the women's various activities. It appeared that, once imprisoned, women were relatively 'free' to pursue a wide variety of activities as long as they organised everything themselves. There were women of all ages and backgrounds, but the solidarity of their political beliefs created a very harmonious working environment.

I listened to their many stories of despair and trauma; their descriptions of rape and torture. Many had witnessed the murder of partners or family members. Some were imprisoned merely because they had been associates of those resisting the military, while others were political activists who openly boasted of justified violence against the Pinochet regime. They were all detained indefinitely under military law and were sceptical about rumoured parliamentary efforts to have them released. In the midst of these awful descriptions of violence and tragedy a group of children from the nearby school suddenly arrived, bringing flowers and baskets of food. The tensions disappeared as mothers, grandmothers and sisters greeted their family members and bustled around to prepare for the main meal of the day. It was the most unexpected experience watching this group of prisoners enjoying their family visitors, who gave the impression that lunch in San Domingo was the most important part of their day. I was told this was a regular routine organised by the nearby Catholic school, where the nuns saw it as their responsibility to cater for the wellbeing of both prisoners and children. It certainly contrasted most favourably with the tightly controlled prison visits that I knew were the norm in Australia.

Leaving San Domingo was more traumatic than entering because I happened to look directly at a soldier patrolling the roof above the passage near the exit. I thought nothing of it, but suddenly he was pointing his machine gun directly at me. I knew it must be only a gesture of defiance so I kept walking, my eyes straight ahead, assuring myself that visiting Australian politicians have a kind of diplomatic immunity from attack. It was such a surreal experience that when I was safely back at our hotel I almost wondered if I had imagined the incident. No doubt it was a symptom of a post-military society in which some members were openly resentful of outsiders who questioned how that administration had flouted international human rights.

That visit to San Domingo Prison made a lasting impression. While I had long advocated women's rights I had never witnessed the intensity of a human rights struggle as experienced by those Chilean women. Within a few years I met one of those inspiring women again. She had been released and was visiting Australia's Parliament to continue recording the experience of those who resist oppression.

CHAPTER 12

Human rights and international politics 1990–1999

THROUGHOUT THE 1990s I became increasingly involved in Parliamentarians for Global Action (PGA) and in international women's networks. I became the Australian representative for PGA, an all-party group concerned with world peace and human rights. Its headquarters in New York was headed by former New Zealand Ambassador, Kennedy Graham. It was a small proactive network of progressive parliamentarians committed to using their influence in global debates. In August 1990, I attended a two day forum in Geneva which coincided with the Fourth Review Conference of the Non Proliferation Treaty. We were briefed on the extension of the treaty to 1995, a comprehensive nuclear test ban, chemical weapons and ballistic missiles verification. On my return, I organised a PGA meeting in Parliament where the Australian Foreign Minister and the ambassadors for the United Kingdom, United States and Russia outlined their policies on amending the Comprehensive Test Ban Treaty.

In 1991, Bob Hawke committed Australian troops to the Gulf War following Iraq's invasion of Kuwait and the subsequent United Nations sanctions. I did not agree with this decision and spoke at a large anti-war rally in Brisbane just prior to the Parliament being recalled in January. A number of colleagues shared my concern that Australia was too readily lining up with our American ally rather than pursuing alternative methods of resolving this conflict. In December of the previous year, I had worked with Queensland Labor colleagues to draft a statement which urged the United Nations to focus on withdrawal of Iraqi troops from Kuwait and demilitarisation of the Middle East. There were tensions among government parliamentarians who wanted to remain loyal to the prime minister but who believed Australia should choose the diplomatic path. In concluding my speech in the Senate I said:

> ... It is my view that even in the midst of this terrible crisis it is still possible for the United Nations to negotiate a ceasefire conditional on the withdrawal of Iraqi troops from Kuwait but enabling independent assessment of border issues. I urge the Australian Government to assert its independence and to maintain its international reputation by offering its skills in diplomacy and arbitration to bring about an immediate cease fire.

Three Labor senators – Bruce Childs, John Coates and I – abstained from the vote to endorse sending troops to Iraq, and subsequently received a letter of reprimand from the ALP National Executive, reminding us of our obligations as government members. In the ALP all members sign a commitment to vote according to the decisions of the caucus majority, but we argued that troops had been committed *before* Labor members had the opportunity to debate the merit of that decision. However, judging from the large number of congratulatory letters I received, there were many people who rejected Australia's involvement in that first Gulf War. It remains a constant source of concern to me that Australian governments continue the tradition of fighting in distant wars regardless of specific national interest. Australian military history should have persuaded us that our size and location is better suited to adopting diplomatic leadership and peacekeeping roles. Instead, our political leaders have followed the British and Americans into conflicts where we would have made a greater contribution by remaining neutral.

Following the Iraq debate, I was the Australian representative invited to attend the Parliamentarians for Global Action forum on the 'New World Order', the post–Cold War era of cooperation proclaimed by Presidents Bush and Gorbachev in Malta in 1989. Arriving in Los Angeles, I found my passport set off an alarm and I was questioned by security staff about the reason for my visit. I produced the invitation and paper for the forum, which was being held on Capitol Hill and hosted by US congressmen. My diplomatic passport did not seem to protect me from rigorous questioning, but I was allowed to continue my journey.

Over thirty members of parliament from twenty-three countries met with US congressional representatives and administration officials for the two-day global dialogue, titled'United nations, the ONLY Super Power', designed to explore the concept of this 'New World Order'. It was at this forum that I was privileged to meet the then Prime Minister of Pakistan, Benazir Bhutto, a charming woman who spoke most eloquently about democratic changes in her country.

A less enjoyable encounter was with a CIA operative who apparently came to the forum to monitor the discussions. When he invited a few of us to dinner one evening we all assumed him to be a hospitable local. He claimed to work with Amnesty International and seemed very interested in our respective countries – Sweden, the Netherlands, Ireland and Australia. Dinner at a local restaurant was pleasant enough until midway through several bottles of wine, when our host suddenly became very aggressive and started berating us for our opposition to the Gulf War. My male companions seemed ready for an all-in brawl but I was keen to retreat back to the hotel. The next day, I checked with the registrations desk to confirm our host's identity, but he was not listed as an official participant. When I queried how he could possibly have entered such a secure location without accreditation, I was told 'Oh those, CIA guys are always snooping around.'

In 1992, I joined a small delegation representing Parliamentarians for Global Action at the Tenth Conference of Heads of State or Government of Non-Aligned Countries in Jakarta. Three parliamentarians from India, the Philippines and Australia joined staff from the New York headquarters. Our group had special observer status personally arranged by Foreign Minister Alitas, who had worked with PGA in developing support for the Non Proliferation Treaty. Our prime task was to meet with as many delegations as possible to lobby for a Parliamentary Information Network on Multilateral Verification for the control of weapons of mass destruction. Such informal contact was designed to prepare the way for debate at the United Nations General Assembly later that year.

The Non-Aligned Summit was a spectacular event with representatives from over sixty nations. Royalty, presidents, prime ministers, foreign ministers and ambassadors all converged on the conference hall, a vast stadium built especially for this occasion. Delegations large and small came with their members in colourful national dress or military uniform, sweeping along the red carpet with bodyguards alert for any sign of obstruction. I watched Palestinian President Arafat's arrival as the media rushed to photograph his every movement, while anxious minders hurried him along to the conference entrance. Police motorcycle escorts worked overtime as lengthy cavalcades of limousines ferried delegates to and from the four-day event.

The opening ceremony featured a welcome by President Suharto followed by the keynote address from UN Secretary General, Boutros Boutros Ghali. The conference focused on the US-declared 'New World Order' and North/South economic polarisation. Much debate centred on economic injustice, especially Third World debt being exacerbated by the manipulation of exchange rates and trading relationships. Many speakers spoke of the need to stabilise the uncertainties of the international monetary system and the World Bank was criticised for failing to reorder its priorities to reduce levels of poverty.

Our delegation was fortunate to meet with several leaders including Mahathir (Malaysia), Alitas (Indonesia), Rao (India) and Wingti (Papua New Guinea). Each of these meetings were very brief, but the fact that we secured even this opportunity reflected the reputation of PGA, which was a constant advocate in international relations. I had urged my colleagues to try to get an appointment with the Prime Minister of Bangladesh, but I was overruled by an Indian colleague who dismissed her by saying: 'No, that would be a waste of time as she is just a simple peasant woman.'

My work with Parliamentarians for Global Action introduced me to colleagues from many different regions of the world and put me in touch with a network of women parliamentarians actively preparing for the United Nations World Conference on Women in Beijing in 1995. While my regular commitments in the Senate and the electorate continued, I was able to focus more on foreign policy and human rights and I became a member of the Joint Parliamentary Committee on Foreign Affairs, Defence and Trade in 1994.

As a result of some of my international work, I was appointed to the Advisory Commission for the Commonwealth Human Rights Initiative (CHRI), a small non-government organisation based in London. It was representative of lawyers, doctors, journalists, trade unionists and parliamentarians who belonged to Commonwealth-wide professional associations. This group had collaborated in a campaign to end apartheid in South Africa during the 1980s and, with the release and subsequent election of Nelson Mandela, had redirected its efforts to campaigning against human rights abuse throughout Commonwealth countries. It established the Commonwealth Human Rights Initiative based at the University of London. Initially, it had volunteer students preparing human rights discussion papers, but over the years it attracted financial support which enabled it to establish a headquarters in New Delhi with a small office in London. The work of CHRI was overseen by a small advisory group representative of different regions of the Commonwealth. We met annually and liaised during the year about key human rights issues to be included in our biannual report to the Commonwealth Heads of Government Meeting (CHOGM).

At my first meeting, I discovered I was the only woman in a group of eminent men from Bangladesh, India, Kenya, Trinidad and the United Kingdom. Some had been government ministers or leading barristers and all were experienced in their understanding of international human rights law. Yet their priorities revolved around civil and political rights with scant attention to economic, social and cultural rights. The rights of women and Indigenous peoples were certainly not on the agenda and by the end of the two-day meeting I was wondering if I was the right person for this group.

However, within the following year a dynamic woman director, Maja Darawula, was appointed to run the office in India and over the next ten years she worked with the Advisory Commission to develop a very professional organisation with a much broader human rights agenda. We focused on education, training and advocacy about United Nations human rights standards in Commonwealth countries. We commissioned experts to write on the ratification of human rights treaties throughout the Commonwealth, and on small arms control, poverty eradication and freedom of information. These reports formed the basis of our lobbying efforts at CHOGM.

In Auckland in 1995, our priority was the suspension of Nigeria from the Commonwealth because of its arbitrary detention of political activists who were trying to protect local tribes-people. Central to the conflict was dispute between the Shell oil company and the Ogoni, whose traditional land was in the Niger Delta where Shell planned a major expansion. Ken Sara-Wiwa, the vocal activist for the rights of the Ogoni, was ill in prison and there were alarming rumours about his safety. Our delegation included Ken Sara-Wiwa's son, Ken Junior, and noted playwright and critic of the Nigerian Government, Sole Wolenski.

Prior to the official CHOGM opening by Queen Elizabeth, CHRI held a press conference which attracted a large number of foreign and local journalists. Everyone seemed to know that the fate of Ken Sara-Wiwa was central to CHOGM's agenda that year; the Nigerian Government was in breach of the Commonwealth's basic commitment to good governance and the rule of law. We met with a number of delegations, urging foreign ministers to insist the issue be placed first on the agenda the following day. But the pace of decision making at these largely ceremonial occasions is slow, so no guarantee could be given. Early the following morning, I received a phone call from a CHRI colleague who had just been told by a distraught Ken Junior that our efforts were too late as his father had been killed the previous evening.

The following day Commonwealth leaders announced that Nigeria would be suspended and the CHOGM censured Nigeria for its extreme action. However, the response was too little, too late and it undermined the Commonwealth's reputation as an organisation committed to the protection of human rights.

By this time, Australia was regarded as a leader in gender policy development so in my work overseas I was able to use our experience to promote these ideas to women internationally. I soon found that, despite historic and cultural differences, women shared the experience of inequality. Whether this related to poverty, violence or representation in decision-making, women could readily identify with the universal imperative to put their human rights on the political agenda.

I was privileged to be an Australian Government representative at both the UN Human Rights conference in Vienna in 1993 and the UN Population and Development Conference in Cairo in 1994. Both events galvanised the international women's movement to focus on gender reform and especially to emphasise that 'women's rights are human rights.' The most controversial aspect of debate at both international events was the question of women's reproductive rights and their ability to determine the size of their families. Official representatives from conservative states and the Vatican were vocally opposed to even the most diplomatic wording of text, which offered women a choice in determining how to control their fertility.

In 1994, I was appointed to the Commonwealth Working Group on Women and Development to prepare a Commonwealth Secretariat position on gender policy planning in all Commonwealth countries. A comprehensive and historic document, which challenged many standing attitudes and practices, was presented in Beijing, giving a commitment on behalf of fifty-four members of the Commonwealth to work with the United Nations to recognise all aspects of women's human rights. It was somewhat ironic that while this forward-looking document reflected a number of Australian legislative and administrative reforms, Australian women themselves were about to witness a scaling back of official government commitment. By March 1996, with the election of the Howard Government, gender policy was downgraded.

In 1995, my mother Jess, older daughter Anna and I went together to the UN's World Women's Conference in Beijing, an event attended by over 30,000 women. We attracted considerable interest from our colleagues as the only three-generation 'delegation.' We stayed together in one room in an inner city hotel enjoying the local cuisine and attending conference sessions each day. Jess and Anna were registered for the NGO conference while I attended the Government conference as a member of the Australian delegation.

Jess had only travelled overseas once before so the trip was especially exciting because at seventy-eight she was able to participate in her first international conference. After a lifetime of promoting recognition of women, she was part of this historic global debate.

Over 500 Australian women attended mainly in the Non-Government forum. UN conferences usually have both official and non-government participation with parallel events and opportunity for the non-government sector to lobby governments to push ahead in adopting more proactive policy. Usually these conferences are run in close proximity so that there is interaction between delegates. However, the Chinese Government was reluctant to engage with hundreds of women activists so the NGO forum was held fifty kilometres from Beijing, in

Huairou. The facilities were minimal as several buildings were incomplete and the heavy rain early in the week created mud and much initial confusion. However despite the distance travelled each day and the challenges women faced it was the NGO forum that maintained fundamental commitment to the international women's reform agenda.

Meanwhile, the Government conference was often bogged down in semantic debate and opposition to the full acceptance of women's rights. Listening to the official speeches of country representatives, many of whom were presidents, prime ministers or ministers, it was easy to imagine that the world's women lived an almost utopian lifestyle. However, it was a very different story at the Non-Government forum where so many women's organisations were there to highlight the harsh reality of women's experience of violence and poverty.

As a result of my involvement with the Commonwealth Expert Working Group on Gender and Development, I was invited by the Women's Committee of the African National Congress to visit South Africa to speak at several gender training workshops. The focus was on combining Australian women's policy development with the Beijing Platform for Action agreed the previous year. Women in the Mandela-led government had tremendous energy and enthusiasm for quickly implementing policy change which recognised women's rights.

The visit was sponsored by AusAid and included Ann Sherry, a former head of Australia's Office of the Status of Women. I flew into Johannesburg late at night and arrived at my hotel to find a welcoming note that my hosts would collect me at 7 am to take me to their national women's conference. I was jetlagged and rather unimpressed with news of the early start to my itinerary but managed a few hours sleep before being greeted the next morning. The group of women talked animatedly about the conference and the several hundred women expected. They told me their president would be there and several important government speakers as well. In my dazed state of mind, I did not really absorb much of this detail but assumed it was going to be a very large women's conference.

We finally arrived at a huge stadium where women were crowding around the entrance. Security was very strict and I watched as several of my companions checked in their small handguns for the day. I still had not guessed the reason for all the excitement and tension in the atmosphere. I was shown into the vast hall and took my place on the stage among several women dignitaries. There was an empty seat beside me and I was told in a most respectful tone that 'you will meet our president soon.' I was beginning to be quite curious about the woman I assumed was the national president of the African National Women's Congress League. I had not met her in Beijing, yet she was obviously held in very high esteem.

Suddenly there was an overwhelming sound of cheering and applause, as my new friend said: 'See, our president has arrived'. I looked down into the audience and watched more than a thousand women stand in colourful unison to pay tribute to the honoured guest. I stared in absolute disbelief as I saw Nelson Mandela himself walking down the central aisle smiling and waving to the crowd. As he approached the stairs up to the platform, the women's powerful voices sang a rousing rendition of the national anthem swaying together in time to the music. I cannot recall a more unexpected and moving experience and by the time this international hero was being introduced to me I was almost speechless.

He sat on my left for a formal welcome and later spoke at length about his vision for South African women. After the official program, we adjourned for tea and he asked me about the mood in Australia as Paul Keating headed into the 1996 election. As Mandela made his farewells he said, 'Tell your Prime Minister I will be thinking of him and hoping he wins – the Australian people have been good friends to us.'

Obviously such a meeting with Nelson Mandela was the highlight of that trip to South Africa. However, there was also an infectious mood for change which continued to inspire me throughout the ten-day visit. I not only met a number of newly elected women parliamentarians in Capetown but had the opportunity to work with groups of women in more isolated regions of the country. One morning I flew to a country town north of Johannesburg where a one-day training session was planned. Women came from near and far, with some walking long distances, to learn about the new recognition of their citizenship. Several of the South African speakers linked the end of apartheid to the urgency for tackling 'gender apartheid', so that future generations of girls would have better lives than their mothers and grandmothers.

When it was my turn to speak, I wondered how to relate my privileged Australian experience to the lives of the women around me. It is never easy, when speaking through an interpreter, to be sure that the key messages are being translated effectively. I chose to use a story based on my local government experience and it brought almost immediate smiles of recognition because it involved women working together to protect their children during the major construction of a new road. During later workshops I found many common themes about health and safety, which had led these women to start taking charge in their own communities.

In 1997, I was selected by my Labor colleagues to spend three months at the United Nations General Assembly in New York. This opportunity was shared with Liberal Senator, Kay Patterson.

Each year the Parliament chooses two representatives to act as Parliamentary advisers to the Australian mission to the United Nations.

I could have just let it be assumed that I was absent on parliamentary business, because my life as a senator and minister had often involved me spending time away from Townsville. However, those times were usually only a few weeks' absence, and I felt I owed my community an explanation about my role overseas. So I issued a press release that included reference to my intended priorities while working at the UN's headquarters in New York. The next day the *Townsville Daily Bulletin* featured me on its front page in a story headlined 'New York Jaunt', complete with a photo of me superimposed on the Statue of Liberty. I was annoyed that Pauline Hanson had been asked to comment on my announcement. Her strident opposition to Indigenous rights and immigration ensured that she would be vocal in her criticism of me working at the United Nations, so all my well-intentioned efforts had been sabotaged.

I muttered to my staff about lodging a complaint with the paper but then I had an idea for turning around this negative publicity. Instead I phoned the editor and offered to write a weekly column from New York so that people could read what I was doing at the United Nations. He not only agreed, but said he would use the 'Reynolds' Statue of Liberty' logo to publicise my column. Called 'Postcard from New York' the column featured a range of news items every fortnight for the next three months (see following page).

The 52nd General Assembly was focused on United Nations reform and ongoing debate about Iraq's compliance with UN resolutions on inspection teams monitoring the destruction of chemical and biological weapons. In addition, there was a myriad of issues being debated within the structure of the six

Image courtesy of Newspix

committee system. I worked with the Third Committee, which is primarily the area of social policy development, including crime prevention, international drug control, advancement of women, refugees, the rights of children, self determination for Indigenous people, human rights, racism, the needs of youth, the elderly, disabled persons and the family. Of special interest was planning for 1999 – International Year of Older Persons.

One evening, Madeleine Albright, then Secretary of State in the Clinton administration, invited us to a special welcome for women working in senior positions at the UN. She told us the story of preparing for this event, admitting her staff had been asked to book a large elegant hall for the reception. However, after checking the invitation list of women representatives she discovered there were only thirty five women, so she had to scale down the planned occasion and find a smaller venue!

It was hard not to notice the male dominance at sessions of the UN General Assembly. At the beginning of each day, the black limousines drove up to the entrance and self-important male leaders and diplomats strode into the building. It was mainly the African men whose bright flowing traditional robes relieved the predictability of the standard grey suit. In the UN General Assembly chamber itself, male speakers came to the podium in relentless succession, so that when a rare woman appeared, we quietly cheered at the all female Australian desk.

On one occasion, during the Iraq debate, I strayed into the Security Council's special briefing session. I had been talking to UN Weapons Inspector, Richard Butler, and somehow drifted along with a crowd of official male delegates registered for that meeting. I was standing at the back of the room when a security officer approached and said:

> Madam, I regret you are not able to remain here as the gentlemen are about to start.

It is true I was not entitled to be at that particular meeting, but I could not help feeling that this exclusion typified the lesser role of women in that UN forum and indeed more generally.

During my time at the General Assembly I was involved in several women's peace conferences to debate the need for greater involvement of women in UN peace missions. At one meeting former congresswoman and staunch women's rights activist Bella Abzug made an impassioned plea for women to try to avoid another war in Iraq. Together with women delegates from Japan, India and Pakistan I presented a proposal to Secretary General, Kofi Annan, on the importance of sending women negotiators to Iraq. We believed there was some opportunity in 1997 for building links with a broad cross section of Iraqi women and that dialogue may have been used to prevent further military conflict. Clearly that proposal was not accepted and several of our UN colleagues dismissed the plan as naïve. However, ten years on after an illegal invasion, many thousands of deaths and an ongoing civil war, it is reasonable to ask: just who was naïve?

CHAPTER 13

'Fair go' politics

THROUGHOUT MY parliamentary career I used my position to provide a voice for vulnerable groups in our community. My work in international human rights advocacy reminded me to look more closely at standards in my own community. It had reinforced my belief that minority groups cannot easily access power to control decisions affecting them unless those with some influence are prepared to speak up for their rights as citizens. Some parliamentarians are deeply committed to this role but others are more inclined to represent those who already have a great deal of influence. I wanted to represent women, not because we are a minority but because our position in society is marginalised and our opportunities are more limited. Coming from North Queensland I was also especially committed to Indigenous rights and my professional life as a teacher ensured I was well aware of social policy affecting people with special needs.

In addition to my work in parliament and with various organisations in Australia and internationally, I was regularly approached by individuals who saw my office as a place of last resort to get some assistance with personal problems that related to their relationship with Federal Government departments. Most of these constituent issues were responded to by my extremely dedicated Townsville staff – Penny Cook, Maureen Balgue, Gary Highland and Jackie Kerr – who patiently listened and then proceeded through the maze of bureaucracy to find solutions. Many constituents passed through my office in half an hour while others returned month after month until some compromise could be found. We also had our regulars, who came mainly for friendly reassurance, and our critics who stormed in very angry about some aspect of Federal Government policy (like the businessman with the tax problem who shouted at me for half an hour but later sent flowers as an apology).

Hundreds of names and faces have long since faded from my memory but some are readily recalled because of the poignancy of their particular stories. One day, an elderly woman came to see me because she had been advised by the Department of Veterans' Affairs that she was ineligible for a war widow's pension because her husband had made unrealistic claims about his war service. Her husband had died only a few months earlier and the insensitive letter from the Department seemed an insult to her husband. She was less concerned about the particular pension than with clearing his good name. Ellen wanted to go through the official appeal process and I got to know her well as we documented her husband's World War 2 service and I heard about his subsequent ill health. Months passed as we tried to gain access to a lost file and detail of a specific war injury.

Finally Ellen confided she would lend me the long treasured evidence to help prove her husband's case. She produced a small heart shaped jewellery box and opened it to reveal the bullet which had been removed from her husband's spine. I knew I could not send this love token off to Canberra as it had been given to her when her husband survived a serious gun shot wound. I decided to seek the advice of a local gunsmith. I had never ventured into a gun shop before but I gave a brief outline of my mission handing over the small silver bullet. The bemused man looked at it briefly and said: 'Sorry, luv, this bullet has never been fired.' He then proceeded to give me a short briefing on identifying spent cartridges and I sheepishly returned the bullet to its box. I left the shop worried about my next move as I knew I could not tell Ellen that this was certainly not the bullet which had caused her husband's spinal injury. But how did we continue the appeals process? I think I had fondly imagined that the bullet's origins could be verified and I could use this to strengthen Ellen's appeal.

The next day I returned Ellen's treasure and advised her that I had not been able to identify the type of bullet so we would simply have to rely on the more recent medical documentation we had gathered. A few months later, we went together to a hearing of her appeal. The three men on the panel were unimpressed with the paper work I had prepared and began asking quite intimidating questions. Only Ellen could respond as I was there as support but could not speak on her behalf. I could see the questioning was upsetting Ellen, and I was concerned she may burst into tears. Suddenly her quavering but defiant voice rang out as she said: 'Well, if you don't believe the doctors I have the bullet with me.' There was silence as she struggled to reach for her handbag. Seconds passed but I could see that the panel members were shifting uneasily in their seats. Then the chairman spoke and kindly assured Ellen: 'Don't worry, that won't be necessary.' I could have hugged him. Ellen won her appeal on the documentation we had provided but more importantly her special secret remained in the jewellery box.

Not all our constituent advocacy was successful and we worked through some very complex personal situations that could not be easily resolved. My introduction to Ted was memorable because he arrived in my office just a few hours after his child had been forcibly removed from his care by Federal Police who had surprised an ordinary Queensland family at the breakfast table that morning. The child was involved in an inter-country custody dispute but these circumstances did not justify the manner in which official processes were followed. This child was taken from the familiarity of the home environment by strangers in uniform. There was no opportunity for explanation and both child and family were treated in an arbitrary manner. A few days later there was a second raid by police, this time to take Ted into custody, where he remained while legal dispute continued about his rights as a father. No charges had been laid because his alleged breach of family law procedures had occurred within another country's jurisdiction, yet he was not released on bail. He was no threat to anyone and his child had already been sent overseas. Finally, my representations to the Attorney General were successful and Ted was released. However, in the process two families had been severely traumatised because proper humane procedures were not followed. Moreover, that child could not return to Australia for almost twenty years.

Many people are shocked to be told there are breaches of human rights in Australia. We like to believe that Australians give everyone a 'fair go' and that human rights violations only occur in other countries where citizens suffer at the hands of brutal dictators. It is disturbing to equate the human rights abuse we see on our television screens with the normal practice of public policy in our own democracy. Yet it was not unusual for me to hear personal stories which indicated that Australia must do much more to protect those individuals and groups that are more likely to face discrimination and harassment. Former Attorney General, Darryl Williams, claimed Australia did not abuse human rights because we do not cut off people's hands, but we have cut off access to justice. Furthermore, a wealthy and stable country like Australia should be setting a higher standard of human rights protection.

Human rights abuse is most likely to occur in institutional settings. It may not start out as calculated abuse but the punitive culture of prisons, detention centres, remand centres and mental hospitals can get out of control unless there is determined oversight by government authorities which have a basic duty of care to those held in the custody of the state.

Over a number of years, I have listened to the stories of prisoners and heard their families speak about the problems in trying to maintain relationships based on impersonal prison visits. I have discussed prison policy with caring officers as well as those who prefer to boast about their 'rough as guts' approach. I have been overwhelmed by the tone of prisoners' letters, which reflect compassion and insight along with anger and despair.

I believe it is time to look at the impact of prison policy on so many Australians and to issue a challenge to politicians to abandon their standard rhetoric of 'getting tough on crime.' It seems the criminal justice system in Australia is indeed tough because there has been a growth in the development of both public and private prisons as more people are imprisoned each year. We seem no closer to overcoming violent crime, yet each year thousands of people are imprisoned for non-violent offences or as fine defaulters. This disrupts families and costs the community millions of dollars that could be better spent in community support. A fresh approach to this dilemma requires political leadership and honesty to face the causes of criminal behaviour and a commitment to generate programs of successful rehabilitation.

Early in my parliamentary career I was phoned by a prison chaplain and asked to visit a young New Zealander gaoled for drug possession while on a working holiday in Australia. He needed advice about a prison transfer so he could serve his sentence in his own country. This single visit was to make a considerable impact on me and generated a long association with the Stuart Prison in Townsville.

In the 1980s it was not easy for me to access prison visiting rights. As a Labor politician questioning the National Party Government I could have been denied entry to this state-controlled institution. Yet finally approval was granted from the Brisbane headquarters and I made arrangements for the local visit. It was unusual for a woman to be 'inside' and there were sniggers, catcalls and furtive glances as I made my way to the interview room. On the way, childish voices called out to me and, as I looked their way, I saw several former pupils – Aboriginal boys whose offences were petty, but their future was unacceptably predictable.

Within weeks of that first visit, my office began receiving letters from prisoners and phone calls from families. My presence within the Stuart Prison had generated enormous interest and high expectations. I had started something I could not ignore and so for the sixteen years of my parliamentary career I found myself acting on behalf of prisoners and their families. Perhaps the most surprising aspect of this association was the fact that on occasions it was actually staff who contacted me to request I visit a particular prisoner.

Stuart Prison has only a comparatively small female section and my office had limited contact with women there. However, there were complaints from women and their families about the pettiness of some of the rules and attitudes. The atmosphere was certainly more homely with some effort to involve the women in a number of work and leisure activities. Yet, because of its size within such a vast male structure, the complaints often focused on discriminatory treatment between male and female units.

This argument was specifically targeted at sports equipment

and activity as well as opportunity for more challenging work experience. Criticism about the way families were regimented for visits and the degrading overuse of strip searches, dominated most of the correspondence I received. The attitude of staff to family visits within the Queensland system seems at best, grudging, and at worst deliberately obstructionist. Similar attitudes existed towards prisoners' correspondence and gifts.

There was no guarantee that correspondence would be received and on one occasion I sent a woman prisoner two copies of my book *The Last Bastion* – one being a personal gift and the other for the library. The theme about women's role in parliament was obviously too much for the staff who refused to pass over the gift until the woman's release several months later. I am still unsure as to the fate of the second copy, but I can only presume the topic was seen to undermine the prevailing philosophy of Stuart Prison. After all, we know equality is a subversive concept.

Pregnant women and mothers of young babies are often resented by other prisoners and staff for 'deliberately' trying to get special treatment. However, the criticism about these 'irresponsible' women hides behind the popular myths. One woman, fearful of the impact of her drug habit on her baby, wrote to me, saying:

> I didn't mean to fall pregnant – well, why would I be that crazy? Its dad doesn't care to know and I was up for being an accessory. But in here everyone thinks I'm lucky because I'll have an easier time. They don't know how scared I am about the birth and whether my baby will be OK. I was mad to do drugs but everyone else did and then it was hard to stop. But I did stop when I knew I was pregnant – I know how easy it is to affect a baby and I want mine to have a chance even if born in prison and when I get out, I will go straight forever to protect my kid from the kind of scum I grew up with.

Throughout my parliamentary career my office continued to receive complaints from Indigenous people about their treatment by police and prison officers. In many cases racism was obvious in the taunts that accompanied physical assault. On other occasions there was differential treatment of Aborigines. For example, on one occasion a young Aboriginal woman was shackled to leave the prison to attend a family funeral. Even some staff were shocked that she appeared to have been singled out for such humiliating treatment.

During the 1990s, Corrective Services Commissioner, Keith Hamburger, brought a more enlightened view to prison administration in Queensland. Yet some of his own officers, parliamentarians and community representatives were sceptical – even hostile – to the reforming advocacy of this senior public servant. His attitudes were unusual because he actually considered that social conditions were often responsible for imprisonment. On one occasion he attracted vocal criticism when he said:

> Jail would never be a deterrent to criminals, especially those from abused families, which showed a lack of understanding of the sub-culture from whence these children have come.

He went on to explain:

> Eight out of ten prisoners serving sentences in excess of five years come from a background of ineffective, neglectful and abusive parenting . . . There was nothing the state could do to these children in terms of punishment that would in any way match the horror already inflicted on them.

This rational plea for a new approach to punishment and rehabilitation was lost in a tirade of verbal abuse with sensational media coverage misrepresenting his goals. Yet it was also in this period that he enabled gradual reform.

Far North Queensland may seem an unlikely venue for a model correctional centre, but Lotus Glen made history in December 1991 when it became the first Australian prison to win a human rights award at the Annual Human Rights and Equal Opportunity Commission's Awards.

I visited Lotus Glen and driving west of Mareeba, an hour from Cairns, you sense the loneliness and isolation that prisoners must feel making their first journey through monotonous scrubland to their place of incarceration. But the sight of the modern façade restored some optimism that this prison may offer a contrast to the grim nineteenth-century model so faithfully transferred from the United Kingdom for use around Australia.

I was more familiar with the stark entrance to Stuart Prison, which reminded me of my first experience of institutional life in Tasmania's Lachlan Park. However, the design of Lotus Glen is reflective of a new, more open approach to prisoner rehabilitation. The correctional centre is built around a garden complete with fountain and has covered walkways connecting the cell blocks, administration, kitchen and laundry. Meal preparation, education, training and leisure programs take place independently in each block. The impression is of a building which could be a modern school or industrial centre.

As I walked around the various units, it was almost possible to forget that this is a maximum security prison. While officers are on duty in each area, there is a degree of informality and individuality which creates its own ambience of trust. Inmates are encouraged to work in pairs or groups to determine their priorities as part of Lotus Glen's self-discipline philosophy.

Of course, Lotus Glen had its share of problems and frustrations and its reputation is not totally free of criticism but the prison adopted a strong commitment to culturally relevant education, music, arts and craft programs. There was a deliberate focus on Aboriginal and Torres Strait Islander culture in building self-esteem among the correctional centre's Indigenous population.

Lotus Glen's success in relating to prisoners' lives was demonstrated by its nomination for the human rights award in 1991. The Aboriginal Legal Service, recognising some genuine reform, made the successful nomination, a tribute in itself to the dedication of staff trying to come to terms with social conditions which see disproportionate numbers of Aborigines and Torres Strait Islanders imprisoned.

The Royal Commission of Enquiry into Aboriginal Deaths in Custody revealed the extent of abuse and mismanagement within the Australian prison system yet despite its recommendations and various efforts by government, the imprisonment rate of Indigenous people remains disproportionately much higher than of the rest of the population. Both families and advocacy groups continue to report disturbing incidents of racist violence and unexplained injury or death in custody.

In 1991, I was appointed as the Federal Government representative on the Council for Aboriginal Reconciliation. This concept – borrowed from South Africa's Truth and Reconciliation process – aimed to heal the political upheaval caused by the polarisation around the establishment of the Aboriginal and Torres Strait Islander Council (ATSIC), the first directly elected representative body established to manage Indigenous programs. The Council for Aboriginal Reconciliation's role was to promote a process of reconciliation between Aborigines and Torres Strait Islanders and the wider Australian community, based on an appreciation and acceptance of Aboriginal and Torres Strait Islander culture and history. The Council had the support of all political parties as it was passed unanimously by both Houses of Parliament.

The Council included twelve Aboriginal representatives, two Torres Strait Islanders and eleven members representing government and opposition, the legal profession, commerce, industry, mining, trade unions, farmers, media, and the ethnic community. Its mandate was to develop a national approach to combating racism and to implement its vision of:

> A united Australia which respects this land of ours, values the Aboriginal and Islander heritage and provides justice and equity for all.

It was an opportunity for Australians to work together across a range of sectors to achieve greater understanding and respect.

The Council's work was just underway when, on 3 June 1992, the High Court handed down its landmark decision in the Mabo case recognising Native Title.

Henry and I had long been aware of our friend Eddie Mabo's struggle for recognition, which had first been an issue in the late 1970s when Premier Bjelke-Petersen had arbitrarily prevented Eddie and his family visiting their ancestral home of Murray Island. After a special Land Rights Conference at James Cook University in 1981, Eddie had begun to compare land rights recognition in the United States and Canada with the myth of *terra nullius* (empty land) in Australia. Working with Henry and a group of lawyers he developed his case which took more than ten years to reach a conclusion.

Throughout the 1980s, I served on the Government Aboriginal Affairs Committee and was disgusted when Labor policy for national Land Rights legislation was abandoned because of the intransigence of then Premier, Brian Burke. Throughout this period I used to comment that Australian Aboriginal Land Rights law would be determined by the High Court, but most people did not know about Eddie's case and were quite dismissive of this idea. Sadly, Eddie died just the year before his appeal was upheld but family members are sure he knew that his life-long struggle had been achieved when the High Court recognised that 'the Murray Islanders of the Torres Strait were entitled to possession, occupation, use and enjoyment of the lands of Murray Island.'

There was a complete overreaction to the Mabo decision especially from the business, mining and farming sectors with extreme claims about Native Title 'taking' urban backyards from ordinary Australians. Sections of the media created a campaign of disinformation which demonstrated a complete lack of interest in understanding the court's decision which simply brought Australia into line with similar countries. The response of many influential people in the community demonstrated their inherent racism by simply failing to see that Indigenous people had as much right to their land through Native Title as other Australians had through freehold title or pastoral lease. On one occasion, a speaker had explained to the audience that mining companies had always accepted responsibility to negotiate with land owners so the High Court decision merely asserted the need for comparable negotiation with traditional owners. A woman immediately stood up and asked incredulously: 'Surely you don't expect us to sit in the dirt and talk to men with bones through their noses.'

In tense negotiations with State Governments, Prime Minister Paul Keating faced strenuous opposition from some of his Labor colleagues. One senior officer reported his Premier's final word: 'Our position on Native Title is minimalist, minimalist like a dot painting.'

Paul Keating saw the historic Native Title ruling as providing a unique opportunity to foster reconciliation, but most state and territory leaders saw it merely as a problem to be overcome.

While the Prime Minister was conducting personal negotiations with Aboriginal representatives late at night in Parliament House, state and territory leaders were mainly reactive in their response. However, after the Native Title legislation was finally passed in December 1993, several State Governments moved motions of support for reconciliation and began to prepare the way to work within the terms of the *Native Title Act*.

The passage of that landmark legislation was one of the most significant occasions in my parliamentary career. Having been closely involved in the campaign for recognition of land rights in North Queensland it was especially gratifying to actually be in the Senate when the legislation passed after so much opposition and tension.

On the night, a film maker asked permission to record the historic moment but unfortunately that request was denied by our political opponents. Consequently, only those of us who were present will always remember the inspiring final hours of debate and the standing ovation in both press and public galleries as the Australian Parliament finally accepted the existence of Native Title. It was indeed a night to remember because there had been such a build up of tension during the months of national hostility towards the High Court decision and to the resulting legislation that followed. The debate itself had been an exhausting experience again because of the extreme views presented.

I wished that Eddie Mabo could have lived to see his dream realised. His ten-year battle with the Australian legal system had certainly earned him the right to witness those monumental changes in Australian land rights law. Eddie and his family had been part of our lives throughout our years in Townsville, so I felt his victory was deeply personal. Despite the racist elements of life in North Queensland, Eddie had triumphed and indeed so had that community because it produced an individual determined to challenge the official racism of successive governments which refused to recognise the traditional owners.

When Pauline Hanson entered the Federal Parliament, a group of her Ipswich constituents approached me to complain about her statement that she would not represent Aborigines. I helped them organise a press conference in Parliament House the week that the controversial new member was officially sworn in as Member for Ipswich. On that occasion the group called upon parliamentarians 'to represent all of their constituents without racial discrimination, fear or favour.' Soon after, I put that notice of motion to the Senate and it was debated and passed unanimously. I don't think the government intended to support it but it was one of those situations where we had a bi-partisan debate and the motion proceeded without dissent.

Over the next six months, Democrat Senator, John Woodley, and I worked to develop the Federal Parliamentarians Code of Race Ethics. We researched the topic but found no special code of ethics which addressed racial discrimination, but we incorporated other parliamentary and industry codes and finalised it for signature in December that year. This Code outlines eight commitments 'to respect the religious and cultural beliefs of all groups living within Australia in accordance with the Universal Declaration of Human Rights.' Initially, it was signed by fifty-seven members and senators at a ceremony in Parliament House which was attended by a broad spectrum of Australia's religious and ethnic community leaders.

In 1997, the Code of Race Ethics was incorporated in the Tasmanian House of Assembly Standing Orders and was endorsed by ten state political leaders: Peter Beattie (Queensland), Bob Carr (New South Wales), Kate Carnell and Jon Stanhope (Australian Capital Territory), John Brumby (Victoria), Mike Rann and John Olsen (South Australia), Geoff Gallup (Western Australia) and

Maggie Hickey (Northern Territory). My office sent the Code of Race Ethics to all 1,435 candidates in the 1998 Federal Election and within a three-week period 553 of them had made a personal commitment to uphold the terms of the code. After the election, I analysed the results and found that 122 members and senators (55%) had pledged to uphold the Code of Race Ethics. Of course there were parliamentarians who indicated they did not support such symbolic commitment of this kind. They said they would be judged by the electorate on their performance rather than a signature on a piece of paper.

Of course that is their prerogative but I think it is also important that elected representatives give a clear commitment that they will not use race or religion to divide the Australian community. Democracy depends on everyone being treated with respect and understanding. The Australian 'fair go' must be more than glib rhetoric.

Federal Parliamentarians Code of Race Ethics

As a member of the Australian Parliament I agree

1. To act in a manner which upholds the honour of public office and the parliament.
2. To respect the religious and cultural beliefs of all groups living within Australia in accordance with the Universal Declaration of Human Rights.
3. To uphold the principles of justice and tolerance within our multicultural society making efforts to generate understanding of all minority groups.
4. To recognise and value diversity as an integral part of Australia's social and economic future.
5. To help without discrimination all persons seeking assistance.

6. To speak and write in a manner which provides factual commentary on a foundation of truth about all issues being debated in the community and the parliament.
7. To encourage the partnership of government and non government organisations in leading constructive and informed debate in the community.
8. To promote reconciliation with Indigenous Australians.

CONCLUSION:

Future politics?

WHEN I LEFT the Senate in June 1999, people asked if I would miss politics. It was not always easy to explain that while I was leaving the Australian Parliament, I had no intention of giving up politics. To me, politics was a way of living, a way of thinking and on occasions a way of acting. I could not see that I would change. In reality, I left one arena of politics to become immediately absorbed in another.

From 1999 until 2005, I was actively involved in promoting the role of the United Nations as National President of the United Nations Association of Australia. My term coincided with a period when United Nations standards were sidelined as the international community focused more on acts of terrorism than the reasons for such extremism. The illegal invasion of Iraq, detention of two Australian citizens at Guantanamo Bay and the treatment of asylum seekers all highlighted the way in which the Australian Government was prepared to sacrifice its international reputation by turning away from international law and practice. During this time I worked through UN agencies to highlight the experience of refugees detained in contravention of the Refugee

Convention and reported to the Commission on Human Rights in Geneva over a three-year period.

I well remember presenting Human Rights Commissioner, Mary Robinson, with enlarged copies of refugee children's drawings which graphically depicted the terror of police behaviour at the Woomera Detention Camp. She was stunned by the violent images drawn by children and questioned the compulsory ID numbers that accompanied each drawing. The following year I met with Sergio Vieira de Mello just months before he was tragically killed trying to establish the UN headquarters in war-torn Baghdad. He was scathing in his comments about Australian refugee policy saying: 'Why is the Australian Government so ruthless towards such vulnerable people?'

Despite the challenge of working internationally, there are aspects of parliamentary life that I do miss. For several months after I left I would automatically reach for the phone to ring the parliamentary library for information. That research and support service is quite unique in providing parliamentarians with quick up-to-date statistics and in preparing well-researched papers on topics of individual choice. I certainly miss being able to comment on a wide variety of subjects in speeches and press releases and having access to the expertise of so many people who appear before parliamentary committees. I do miss the privilege of being part of a Labor Government which enabled me to contribute to policy development and a genuine social reform process. I must admit, it is also frustrating to lose the ability to work directly with the prime minister or specific ministers to try to influence the direction of new policy.

However, most of all, I miss the people and the excitement of the unpredictable in parliamentary politics. There are not many jobs where every day is different. Although some routines remain when Parliament is sitting because elected representatives are locked in to the parliamentary schedule from early morning until night, there is no certainty about which issues will be the focus of debate or behind-the-scenes manoeuvring. The comparison of Parliament with life in a boarding school is quite accurate because in Canberra there is very little time for life outside the big house on the hill when Parliament is in session. A normal day may start with breakfast meetings and finish well beyond midnight.

When I am asked for my fondest memories of life in Parliament House I remember the camaraderie of friends on all sides of politics. It is often said that there are few friends in politics because of the extremely competitive and volatile nature of parliamentary life. However, many close friendships do manage to withstand those pressures. Furthermore, parliamentarians celebrate many special occasions together when for a brief time the tensions of politics are forgotten. I remember a particular Christmas party in Old Parliament House when I went first to the office of Deputy Prime Minister and Attorney General, Lionel Bowen. It was a lively occasion and I stayed for some time until suddenly someone said: 'Hey, we mustn't forget Bob's party.' The Prime Minister's office was just down the corridor so the entire party marched down to his party, led by Lionel, as we all sang the socialist anthem 'The Red Flag.' I am not sure that today anyone would know the words and anyway, socialism does not rate in opinion polls.

After another party the following year, a group of us decided to move the portraits in King's Hall. It had not escaped our attention that the only two women to be exhibited were Dame Enid Lyons (Liberal) and Dorothy Tangey (Labor), the first women elected to the Australian Parliament. But both their portraits were obscured behind solid columns at the rear of the hall. This was unacceptable and we definitely thought they should be featured at the front. Several members of the Status of Women Committee struggled to lift the heavy gilt framed pictures until some of our male colleagues offered to help. When the images of two former prime ministers were safely placed behind the columns we stood to applaud the pioneering women who now overlooked the entrance to King's Hall.

However the next day we were surprised to find there had been an official rearrangement and poor Enid and Dorothy had been returned to obscurity. Senator Ruth Coleman raised the issue with President Doug McClelland in Question Time and after that incident there was a general rotation of all portraits so our women had the opportunity to be more prominent. I wonder how many more years it will take before a woman prime minister's portrait is displayed in the gallery of Australian leaders?

While parliamentarians are often seen as aloof and serious, they need a sense of humour to survive as many people are quick to criticise and ridicule their often well-intentioned efforts to improve community life. When Bob Hawke's Government was newly elected there was a general expectation that pension rates would increase but a number of lobby groups continued to present their case for reform. The National Council for the Single Mother and her Child invited all parliamentarians to a luncheon party on the lawn opposite Old Parliament House and about twenty of us accepted. When we arrived we found a long trestle table completely set for a formal three-course meal. We were asked to be seated so the children could serve us. I expected that the cheapest possible food would be provided to highlight the only kind of meal that could be bought on a low pension. However the women had been much more strategic (and mischievous!) in communicating their message.

The meal was exactly the same as that served in the subsidised parliamentary dining-room: soup, meat with three vegetables followed by strawberries and cream. However the portions offered were so small they were impossible to manage. There we sat – a group of new young politicians keen to improve the standard of living for people on low incomes. We were surrounded by the media as we tried to scrape a taste of soup from a virtually empty bowl. I remember the single pea that sat in the middle of my plate with a tiny sliver of meat and a teaspoon full of mashed potato. Finally I was presented with a quarter of a small strawberry and a speck of cream. The message was even more effective because the children took their duties very seriously and it was clear this meal was meant to offer food for thought rather than any sustenance.

That protest highlights the importance of combining humour with an illustration of double standards in public policy. Too often parliamentarians and public servants make pronouncements affecting people's lives which they certainly would not accept for themselves. One of the problems of parliamentary life is that it can separate people from the reality of most people's experiences and that in turn can lead to unrealistic policy.

Many parliamentarians are forced to leave parliament because the voters or their political party have decided it is time for a change. I was one of those who was to able to choose my time of departure. Looking back over my sixteen year parliamentary career I realise just how privileged I was to enjoy all those years when there was a mood for reform in Australian politics. So many of the issues I worked to promote relied on an understanding of social justice accepted by a majority of people. However during my last three years I was able to contrast that experience with being in opposition at a time when there seemed a determination to scale back so many policy commitments of the Hawke/Keating years.

During the first term of the Coalition Government I watched the systematic undermining of gender policy initiatives, Native

Title, multiculturalism and human rights. Australia adopted reactionary language about vulnerable groups with senior ministers boasting 'an end to political correctness.' I have never understood why people parrot that illogical term in such a dismissive way. Those of us who had worked so hard to ensure that marginalised groups were included in policy development suddenly found that these ideas were considered out of date and it was no longer necessary to include or offer specific support for all Australian citizens.

In reflecting on my own experience of parliamentary politics I cannot help but wonder how much has changed for those women who have been elected more recently. I was amazed to see that thirty years after local media insisted on photographing me in traditional pose as a housewife, Julia Gillard's kitchen could become the subject of national debate. I cannot imagine any journalist questioning the Prime Minister about the last time he prepared a meal in the Kirribilli kitchen.

Women in politics still suffer what Carmen Lawrence has ascribed to the 'Madonna or whore' syndrome. The double standard illustrated in this phrase persists in our parliaments and it remains a challenge for women leaders to be fully accepted. Aggressive, outgoing women are suspected of being too like their brawling male colleagues. There is no greater threat to some men than a vocal woman determined to match their abrasive style. Yet those women who choose a more cooperative style are often bypassed because they are not seen as ruthless enough to participate in those inevitable power struggles.

I find it difficult to offer useful advice to younger women considering a political career. I have been exceptionally fortunate in juggling my family and career over more than four decades but I am reluctant to boast that it is an easy course for others to follow. Many women do sacrifice their personal relationships or find it difficult to combine parenting with their role in the workforce. It is doubly difficult to manage a political career with family life. Sections of the community apply such blatant double standards to women who choose a less traditional path. The highly successful young woman mayor of Launceston, Janie Dickenson, was constantly criticised for taking her baby son to council events. Yet had she installed a nanny or placed him in child care her opponents would have been equally strident.

Women leaders who choose not to have children are also vulnerable to unfair scrutiny. Recent extremist comments about Julia Gillard indicate that some ageing misogynists can't accept women parliamentarians without defining them by their gender.

I am fairly philosophical about the way our lives evolve. At a Women in Leadership colloquium at Harvard's John F Kennedy School of Government we were asked to comment on the reasons for our successful careers. The majority of us outlined key turning points but referred back to luck and favourable opportunity as the foundations for these turning points. Our seminar leader chided us saying that in her experience of running similar training sessions, men are more likely to list their qualifications and achievements. It is an interesting gender difference to try out on unsuspecting colleagues and friends.

Women are still more likely to have reservations about venturing into public life because they understand both the personal and the professional risks. It is much harder to control the direction of a political career and some of the consequences may not be acceptable. However, all life choices are a gamble so I would always urge women to 'give it a go' and choose the path that seems right for them. Women have no reason to feel guilty about their choices and it is important we resist some of the remnants of misogyny, which persist in both the public and the private sphere. Most women in relationships heading towards a political career need partners whose egos are not challenged by the prospect of women's success. While political partners of both sexes can resent the high profile of their partners, it is men who are more likely to feel challenged or affronted if their partner's career overshadows their own. Recognising this and dealing with it early on can allay sensitivities which can occur in any partnership.

Despite the best laid plans it can be a delicate balance. The community tends to assume that in electing their parliamentary representative they have actually elected a political couple. The partners of male politicians are often expected to assume a double workload but the role of women's partners is less clear. I remember that when I became prominent in Labor politics it affected Henry's status as an independent political commentator because everyone assumed he must automatically adopt my views. One day while he was offering his professional assessment of a state election campaign on talkback radio, an antagonistic caller rang to accuse him of bias because he was married to that Margaret Reynolds. Henry took a deep breath and responded 'Madam, I can assure you I am my own person.' On the other hand there was one famous occasion during the heated Native Title debate when I was accused of adopting my particular stance only because I took advice from that 'Mabo historian'! Certainly I believe we operated as a particularly effective political team; I was often able to access ideas and information from Henry but I had the opportunity to translate them into policy and practice.

It is not easy for politicians to engage Australians in an easy-going dialogue about politics because too many people are often suspicious and disparaging of a system they do not understand or trust. These attitudes are easily fostered by irresponsible sections of the media which have an unfortunate tendency to highlight either conflict or trivia. The televised images of the raucous verbal power-play between government and opposition gives the impression of competitive sport rather than rational debate about how our society should function. The dominance of testosterone in our Parliaments alienates all those who want to see their representatives tackling serious policy options without the malicious jousting that overshadows serious analysis. Sometimes the atmosphere of Question Time is more like a football grand final than a realistic debate to ensure government is fully accountable.

There are those who are enthralled by the theatre of parliamentary debate, but for many observers the constant abuse and gamesmanship merely reinforces cynicism about the democratic process. There is equal resentment about the way in which some political debate is too controlled, with comment reduced to bland sound bites that are really meaningless. It is difficult to get a balance which effectively engages the public. I remember my predecessor Jim Keeffe assuring me 'you can please some of the people some of the time but you can't please all of the people all of the time.'

There is little doubt that the media is largely responsible for selecting the issues that will be presented to Australian households on a daily basis. Some journalists use their investigative and analytical skills to cut through the efforts of political spin doctors and this professionalism is to be applauded. However, if the electorate is sceptical about politics we need look no further than the way sections of the media trivialise and misrepresent important aspects of public debate. This in turn scares off our elected representatives who then rely on carefully crafted press releases to remain 'on message.'

During the last ten years there has been a concerted attack on public debate that questions Federal Government policy. Ministers deride the 'intellectual elite' as being remote from the experience of 'ordinary Australians.' This has created a mood of social conservatism in which too many parliamentarians are reluctant to challenge the current official line. Political comment has become cautious and predictable, manipulated by those who want to control the release of public information and the direction of community debate. The stage management of Australian politics has disillusioned many and in the process excluded a range of opinions. Sometimes it seems that only the cartoonists can show us the world as it really is. The political agenda has become dominated by a mean-spirited manipulation of issues that encourages many Australians to retreat into their own lives apparently more concerned with personal than public priorities.

We need to encourage much more collective thinking and action about the kind of society we want to leave behind for our children and grandchildren. Getting involved in decisions that will affect them is the responsibility of all citizens, not just those who currently represent us. Perhaps we all need to take to heart the words of Martin Luther King who said:

> Our lives begin to end the day we become silent about things that matter.

Acknowledgements

I WANTED TO write the story of my experience of politics as a woman who got involved because of issues that were important to me. Many people are cynical about politicians and their contribution to public policy while others simply see the whole democratic process as boring and irrelevant. I have tried to show that politics is about all of us and the kind of society we want. It is not just about party politics or parliamentary politics, but the politics of grassroots participation where people can use their collective ideas to achieve better opportunities for everyone. This book is especially about the changing roles of women and men over the last forty years. I hope it may encourage more people to get involved in political debate and activism.

There are far too many friends and colleagues to name in acknowledging those who have given me support and encouragement over the years but there are just a few who have made an important contribution to the preparation of *Living Politics*. I would like to recognise John Iremonger who first proposed the idea of this political memoir. The guidance of Vyv Winter, who read a draft manuscript, was important in getting me started.

To Rosie Fitzgibbon, Anna Crago and Wendy Sanderson of University of Queensland Press and Editor Sharon Neville, many thanks for your patience and helpful comments. I am indebted to Lyndell George, Elizabeth Foxcroft and Jean Willoughby who typed my ever changing text.

Finally my special thanks to family and colleagues whose stories I have included without fear or favour!

INDEX